What EVERY GIRL *Should Know*

A Study in ...

Love

Life

& Faith

Written by **Myklin Cox**

Artwork by Katherine Lindholm

What Every Girl Should Know ...*A Study In Love, Life and Faith*

ISBN: 1-59571-025-6
Library of Congress Number: 2004107961

What Every Girl Should Know
PO Box 132
Maize, KS 67101-0132

Back Cover Photo Credit: Riverside Photography

This Book Belongs To:

_____

Date:

_____

Dedicated to my best
Friend in the Universe . . .
Jesus Christ.

I can't wait to spend all of forever with You!

CONTENTS

Acknowlegements

Wendy...
What an awesome woman of the Lord you are! It was your vision that first inspired me
to give something like this a shot. Somewhere along the way the Lord gave me a vision
for this as well! You and your family are such blessings to me. ☺

Katherine...
How you have amazed me with your flexibility and skill as you've worked
so graciously on this project with me! What can I say? Your artwork is simply perfect.
Thank you for the spirit of pure joy the Lord has given you
and the sweet way you always share His love. ☺

Dad...
You are my rock and an ever-wise counselor! It's great working with and learning
so much from you in the office! Thank you for loving me in spite of *me*,
and encouraging me to be all God wants me to be. No matter what,
you'll always have my heart and my love! ☺

Mom...
Sometimes I wonder why God allowed such a wonderful woman as *you*
to be my precious Mother and sweet, sweet friend! Thank you for your servant's heart,
years of training, and hours spent on your knees in prayer for all of us.
You are a tremendous calm in the midst of the storms of life and I love you. ☺

Marc...
Your incredible faith and great friendship always inspires and encourages me.
How could I ask for a better older brother? I'm excited to see where God will lead you
as you follow Him down this road of ministry! While you're serving in a far away place
someday, always remember your little sister loves you "oodles and gobs."☺

Logan...
Wow! Can you believe we used to fight like cats and dogs when we were little?!
Looking at you now, I see a young man full of character and love for the Lord.
You have an awesome sense of humor that never ceases to make me smile!
I thank God for you, my precious "big-little" brother. I will always love ya buddy! ☺

My Lord and Savior Jesus Christ...
I owe You my very life!! How can I thank You enough for dying on the Cross for such a
wicked and sinful heart as my own? May I learn to love You as much as You love me!

Well, hi! Myklin here, just dropping you a note as you begin this journey through *What Every Girl Should Know.* I can hardly believe that I have the awesome privilege of sharing a few of the things I have discovered from my own life with you. Many of these things I have learned through trial, and me oh my...*so* much error! ☺ This study may be called *What Every Girl Should Know,* but in all honesty, I'm still working on taking some of these things to heart myself! So, that's why it will be fun to go through this *together.* ☺

Every girl will eventually grow up. When that happens, we hope we have learned the necessities of life to be able to make it in this world. A wise girl will learn these lessons while she is still young. Making it in this world does *not* mean being successful in what we do, becoming well liked or popular, wearing the latest styles, or having the finer things in life (as our world often thinks). In and of themselves, these things aren't bad to have—in fact they're very nice! However, I believe that making it in this world means knowing the appropriate words to speak at the appropriate time, striving to have a beautiful heart rather than an impressive outward appearance, loving the people in our lives that are the hardest to love, and most importantly, having a right relationship with Jesus Christ. That is the reason I wanted to share this study with you today – so that you may understand beyond a shadow of a doubt what this life is really all about.

So my friend, I'm praying for you! May you be able to draw close to the Lord and may He make Himself real to you in ways you cannot even imagine as you make your way through this course!

It doesn't matter who you are! You are special to *Him,* and that makes you special to *me.* So, from my heart to yours, may God richly bless you! ☺

Your Friend,

Myklin ☺

P.S. You pronounce my name "Mike-Lynn"! ☺

As We Begin...

➤ Take a few minutes to think about what matters most to you in your life. Is it what your friends think of you, or the way you look? Do you strive to please *yourself* more than others?

➤ Write a few of your thoughts down about this course in the space below. Maybe you'd like to set a goal for yourself throughout the weeks ahead. Perhaps you need to ask the Lord to help you be more like Him, or maybe you've never asked Him into your heart to begin with. Please just take a moment to reflect on what's truly in your ♥.

_____

_____

_____

_____

_____

_____

_____

_____

_____

_____

What Should Every Girl Know?

Chapter 1 - She should _know_ and believe in her heart that Jesus Christ loves her and has a wonderful plan for her life. *(1 John 5:20)*

✄ ✄

So, have you heard the Good News about Jesus?? He loves you and wants to be a part of your life!
This chapter is basically the Gospel of Jesus Christ in a nutshell. ☺

Chapter 2 - She should _know_ her Savior better by the daily reading of His Word, praying with Him and meditating on His precepts. *(Isaiah 58:2)*

✄ ✄

Do you make time for Jesus? How do you know what to pray for and how to go about doing it?
Well, let's take a look and find out. ☺

Chapter 3 - She should _know_ that her body belongs to God and should strive to be pleasing on the inside, as well as on the outside. *(1 Corinthians 6:19)*

✄ ✄

Here's the scoop on your outward appearance. We'll discuss health, hair care, hairstyles,
facial shapes, makeup, and clothes! ☺

Chapter 4 - She should _know_ how to look for good character in the people she chooses to spend time with and treat as role models. *(James 4:4b)*

✄ ✄

Do you know the importance of good friendships? Learn how you can become a good friend, exhibit good manners,
and discover Who the best role model of all time is. ☺

Chapter 5 - She should _know_ that she has been given talents and abilities by God as a way to bless those He will bring across her path. *(Ephesians 1:18)*

✄ ✄

Have you ever thought about what's so special and totally unique about YOU?
Let's talk about using whatever abilities God has blessed you with to bless others! What about basic household skills
like cooking, baking and sewing? Don't worry...we'll discuss those, too! ☺

Chapter 6 - She should _know_ that her life is in the Lord's Hands and His timing is always perfect. *(Job 42:2)*

✄ ✄

Let's talk about how God works in our hearts and lives. What about your future, the hard times ahead,
and life callings? And how do you treat guys NOW while you're trying to figure them out and be their friends,
yet not quite ready for marriage? Well...let's find out! ☺

Chapter 1

ಐ ೞ

She should <u>know</u> and believe
in her heart that
Jesus Christ loves her
and has a wonderful plan
for her life.

ಐ ೞ

"And we <u>know</u> that the Son of God is come, and hath given us an understanding, that we may <u>know</u> Him that is true..." ~ 1 John 5:20 (KJV)

ॐ ೞ

Some Good News

Even though I may not personally know you, I already know something about you. What is that you ask? I know you have been created by God's own Hand and that He has a *very* special purpose in mind for you. The Creator of the universe has a plan for *you* and for *me*. This fact has never ceased to blow my mind!

People all around the world today are trying to tell us that God is *not* important and that He definitely *doesn't* have anything to do with real life. No doubt you've heard things like "Be your own boss" and "*You* can do anything *you* put your mind to." These messages are everywhere you turn! Well girls, I'm here to tell you that God has *absolutely everything* to do with real life, and more than that, *your* life! ☺

When I was younger, I remember people telling me how special I was to God and how much He loved me. This caused my mind to fill with questions that I so desperately needed the answers to! I used to wonder *why* I was so special to Him. Why did He create me? How could someone like *me* be special in God's eyes?

11

For the answers I sought, I could only turn to one place: The Bible, God's Holy Word. These verses from Scripture explained so much to me...

"This is real love. It is <u>not</u> that we loved God, but that <u>He</u> loved us and sent His Son as a sacrifice to take away our sins." ~ 1 John 4:10 (NLT)

"For God so loved the world that He gave His one and only Son, that <u>whoever</u> believes in Him shall not perish but have eternal life." ~ John 3:16 (NIV)

"That if you confess with your mouth, 'Jesus is Lord,' and believe in your heart that God raised Him from the dead, <u>you will be saved</u>." ~ Romans 10:9 (NIV)

"[God] has saved us and called us to a holy life — not because of anything we have done but because of His own <u>purpose</u> and <u>grace</u>." ~ 2 Timothy 1:9a (NIV)

These were the answers the Lord knew I needed! I could see what He wanted from me. He had *chosen* to love me even before the world began, but not because He thought that I was such a wonderful person or anything like that. Even though He loved me, there was still a problem. My sin had separated me from spending eternity with God. True, I hadn't committed what so many people call "big, bad sins", but it didn't matter! The sins I *had* committed (seemingly big or small) deserved *death* according to Romans 6:23. That meant I was doomed for eternity.

But, the story doesn't end there! Yes, I *would* have been eternally doomed had not God sent His only Son Jesus to live a perfectly sinless life here on earth. He died in *my* place on the cross and rose again on the third day! He paid the penalty for my sin by dying for *me.*

Such a realization was both freeing and convicting for me! Why would someone give His own life...for me? Jesus Himself said in John 15:13, *"Greater love hath no man than this, that a man lay down his life for his friends." (KJV)* Wow!! It was because of His great love that He lay down His life for me!

What an amazing love and humongous sacrifice Jesus gave on my behalf! All He asked of me was to simply confess Him as Lord, and believe in Him as the only Son of God. If I did this, the Bible said that *I would be saved!!* ☺

So that's just what I did! I asked Jesus to come live inside of my heart and to forgive me of my sins. He did exactly what He said He would do and I have *never* been the same!

Now my reason for living is not to acquire all the things this world has to offer. In the end, these earthly treasures will only fade away. That's why I'm striving to live a holy life that pleases the Holy God who loves me. When my life here on earth is over, I will just be starting my life in Heaven with Jesus!

What about *you?* Do *you* have a reason to live? Have you stopped to think about where you will be spending eternity? God's love is available to anyone who will accept it. He's sitting with His arms wide open, waiting to welcome you into His family if you'll just believe and accept Him into your heart! Trust me when I say Jesus Christ will make *all* the difference in the world!

Again, what does this have to do with what every girl should know? Well, I believe the *very first thing* every girl should know is that there is an open invitation to accept the Lord Jesus as her own personal Savior. Each lesson in this course from here on out will build upon this concept.

Everything that truly matters in this life must *start* with a relationship with Jesus Christ! Nothing else truly matters when you think about what He did for you and how He wants to spend eternity with *you!* ☺

Oh girls, how I pray that you already know Him and that you are seeking His will for your life! If you have never given your life to Jesus, then I encourage you to give it a lot of thought. It is *the most important* decision you will *ever* make in your life! We simply don't know how much time we have here on this earth. That's why we should live every day as if it will be our last...making a difference for eternity...sharing God's love with those we meet...and trying to love HIM as much as HE loves US.

> *So please, don't wait to make a decision to follow Christ!*
> *Trust me...it's the best decision you will ever make in your life.*

TIME TO THINK!

1. How much sin must someone commit in order to condemn them to live eternally separated from Jesus?

_____

_____

2. Write Ephesians 2:8-10 on the lines below:

_____

_____

_____

_____

3. Based on these verses, how are we saved?

_____

_____

4. Does Jesus want to have a relationship with us because of our great character qualities? Why or why not?

_____

_____

_____

5. Why do you think some people don't want to have a relationship with Jesus?

_____

_____

_____

6. Have *you* ever invited Jesus to come live inside *your* heart? Why or why not?

_____

_____

_____

What About Me?

1. What matters most to me in life? (Hint: The best way to find this out is to consider what you are constantly thinking about, what the center of your conversation is, what makes you smile, etc.)

_____

_____

_____

_____

2. Do I find myself being concerned with simply my *own* happiness and fulfillment rather than the happiness and fulfillment of others?

_____

_____

_____

3. Can I say that I have true joy in my life on an everyday basis? Why or why not?

_____

_____

_____

4. If I were to die tonight, do I know for sure that I would go to Heaven?

       Yes   No

5. Am I ready to trust Jesus with my life?

       Yes   No

☐ **Yes, I will ask Jesus Christ to come into my heart and be my Lord and Savior...*TODAY!***

*Signature / Date:*_____

Asking Jesus into your heart and life today is as simple as ABC... ☺

A.B.C.

Admit you're a sinner.

Believe Jesus died on the cross and rose again on the third day.

Confess with your mouth Jesus is Lord.

The Bible says that Jesus knows our thoughts before we can even voice them. He knows the deepest needs of our hearts and He longs to answer them! That's why it doesn't take anything fancy or special to begin a relationship with Jesus Christ today!

Simply be honest about your failures, let Him know that you believe He is the risen Son of God, and admit how much you need Him in your life. If you are sincere and true about this in your heart, then the Bible says:

> *"That if you confess with your mouth, 'Jesus is Lord,' and believe in your heart that God raised Him from the dead, <u>you will be saved</u>. For it is with your <u>heart</u> that you believe and are justified, and it is with your <u>mouth</u> that you confess and are saved... For, 'Everyone who calls on the name of the Lord <u>will be saved</u>.'"*
> *~ Romans 10:9,11 & 13 (NIV)*

Dear friend, how I pray you will not wait a moment longer to ask the Lord Jesus Christ to come and live inside your heart.

He loves you more than you could ever know.

Chapter 2

ৡ ৎ

She should <u>know</u> her Savior better by the daily reading of His Word, praying with Him & meditating on His precepts.

ৡ ৎ

"Yet they seek Me daily, and delight to <u>know</u> My ways..."
~ Isaiah 58:2 (KJV)

A Quiet Time

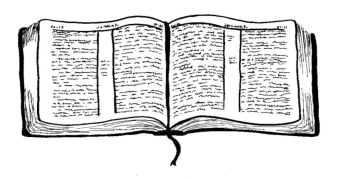

Do you know what it means to have a Quiet Time? Maybe you have visions of sitting in a corner all by yourself after doing something you shouldn't have, considering the consequences of your actions and vowing *never* to do *that* again! That would be known as a "time out", *not* a Quiet Time. ☺

A true Quiet Time involves interaction between you and God. This is a portion of your day set aside for you to pour out your heart to your Savior and to hear what He has to say to you!

So often we rush around like headless chickens trying to accomplish everything on our long to-do lists! ☺ There's much to be said for simply setting a few moments aside every day and filling it with nothing but the sound of your heart communicating with the heart of your Heavenly Father!

There are three steps you need to take for a proper Quiet Time:

STEP 1: Study His Word

STEP 2: Pray With Him

STEP 3: Meditate on His Precepts

Step 1
Study His Word

Once you have given your heart and life to Christ, this next step is *very critical.* I would encourage you to do this one thing every single day.

When I was eleven years old, someone challenged me to make a commitment that I would read at least 5 minutes out of the Bible every day. I decided to take the challenge, and that one habit has changed my life in more ways than I could have ever imagined! Why don't *you* spend time praying, reading, and meditating on what God has to say in His Word? It's not like you have to read the entire Book in one week. You could start small to begin with and let God do the rest! ☺

In this next section, I've included the outlines I use in my Quiet Time to give you some helpful ideas. Experiment with your own style. I'm telling you, He *will* bless you for taking the time to be with Him. I can't say it enough. Please, please, please...read your Bible *every day!* ☺ Next to knowing Christ as your Savior, this could make more of a difference in your life than anything else we will discuss in this course. But, that's only if you take the challenge. So...*will you?*

Let's look more closely at each of these three steps! ☺

Today's Date:_____

Passage of the Bible I read:

_____

Key verse(s) and what this means to me:

_____

_____

_____

_____

Step 2
Pray With Him

When we pray, we need to keep in mind that we are not just talking *to* God, but also talking *with* God. He's not some sort of cosmic slot machine popping out answers to all the prayer requests we have! ☺ When we pray, we need to keep four things in mind. An easy way to remember these four parts of prayer is to think of the word: ACTS.

Adoration: *Spend time praising God for who He is. (Love, Mercy, Justice, etc.)*

Confession: *Confess your faults to Him, asking Him to show you sin in your life.*

Thanksgiving: *Thank Him for all of the blessings He has given you.*

Supplication: *Share your needs and the needs of others with Him.*

Prayer should be a vitally important part of every Christian's life! But prayer doesn't have to be at any set time, or in any set form. Yes, we should *always* adore Him, confess our sins, give thanks, and offer supplication. But what if you only have time for a prayer with just a few words? Will God hear your prayer, no matter how small or large? Yes! The Bible says in 1 Thessalonians 5:17 that we should *"pray without ceasing"!* This means that we *always* need to have a heart of prayer and an open line of communication with our Heavenly Father. You can talk with God 24 hours a day, 7 days a week. He's with you when you get up every morning, as you do your school or chores during the day, when you're falling asleep at night, and every time in between! Your Heavenly Father even hears small prayers like, *"Lord, I need You right now"* or, *"Jesus, please give me strength!"*

He may choose to help you in a way that is different than you would like. You may or may not see it, but He will *always* answer. He may say, "Yes", "No", or "Wait a while". However He responds, rest assured that He *will* answer your prayers! So go ahead and talk with Him, and then step back and let Him work in your life! ☺

Adoration & Praise:

_____
_____
_____
_____

Conviction & Confession:

_____
_____
_____
_____

Thanksgiving:

_____
_____
_____
_____

Supplication:

_____
_____
_____
_____

Prayer Requests:

_____
_____
_____
_____

Step 3
Meditate on His Precepts

Why is this last step so important? When you meditate on something, you think about and ponder on it. You can meditate on all sorts of things throughout the day, such as the way you look, how you feel, or even what yummy things you'd like to eat for lunch. *(You know, all those really "important" things!)*

God wants us to meditate on *His* precepts and *His* principles. Do you know why? Because when we fill our minds and hearts with promises from His Word, we are saturating ourselves with Him! Our minds and hearts are being filled with thoughts of our Heavenly Father, and not the silly things of this world! ☺

When we are faced with a difficult situation, we can become tempted to respond in a way that isn't very Christ-like. Being able to draw on His Word for strength is the *best* thing we can do in these situations!!

That's why during my Quiet Time every morning I write on an index card my purpose for the day, along with verses to encourage me. I put that card in my pocket or purse and carry it with me the rest of the day! Then, when I get overwhelmed or discouraged at some point during the day *(which is bound to happen...believe me! ☺)*, I simply pull out my card and read those verses from God's Word. I love being able to turn to my Heavenly Father for a Word of encouragement straight from Him!

<u>Here are a few helpful hints:</u> *Memorize key verses of Scripture! That way they will always be written on your heart and you can take them with you wherever you go. Also, fill your whole life with God's Word! Write verses on sticky notes and put them in places you will see often, or frame verses and hang them on a wall. Put some thought into it and see what other great ideas you can come up with! ☺*

My Purpose For the Day:

_____

Verses to remember when I get discouraged today:

_____

_____

_____

Above all other relationships in this world, your relationship with Jesus Christ is the *most important!* I cannot stress enough how vital it is to be in the Word of God on a daily basis. God *wants* to spend time with you. He's crazy about you, ya know! ☺ He wants to be your first thought in the morning, your song during the day, and your last smile as you fall asleep. If Jesus Christ was *first* in your life, who knows what awesome things He could have in store for you?! ☺

> *"You are the salt of the earth. But what good is salt if it has lost its flavor?*
> *Can you make it useful again? It will be thrown out and trampled underfoot as worthless.*
> *You are the light of the world - like a city on a mountain, glowing in the night for all to see.*
> *Don't hide your light under a basket! Instead, put in on a stand and let it shine for all.*
> *In the same way, let your good deeds shine out for all to see, so that everyone*
> *will praise your Heavenly Father." ~ Matthew 5:13-16 (NLT)*

This passage tells us that we are the salt and the light in this lost and dying world! To have a fulfilled life (and by that I mean one with true joy, true peace, true love, and true contentment), we must be willing to give God every bit of ourselves. It may be uncomfortable to share our faith with a lost friend, to get up earlier to have a Quiet Time, or to pray every evening before bed. However uncomfortable those things may be, we must be *willing* to give them up to the Father of all. When we do this, He is then able to use us as His salt and light!

When it comes to sharing our faith with others and being bold witnesses in this world, we have to kiss our fears goodbye. I know it's easy to say and very hard to do, but the rewards are *countless* and far more valuable than you can ever imagine. The nervousness we feel may never leave, but we must *always* remember that *His* strength is *perfected* when we are at our weakest moments!!

> *"But He said to me, 'My grace is sufficient for you,*
> *for My power is made perfect in weakness.'" ~ 2 Corinthians 12:9a (NIV)*

Believe me when I say that He can give you the strength to do *whatever* it is He has called you to do when the time comes. ☺ Philippians 4:13 says that you can do *all* things through Christ! So...will you give yourself completely to *Him?*

TIME TO THINK!

1. Do you have a Quiet Time every day? Why or why not?

_____

_____

_____

2. How would it make you feel if someone you love very much went for an extended amount of time without talking or spending time with you? Would you consider someone like this a true friend if his or her behavior never changed?

_____

_____

_____

_____

3. Based on your answer above, how do you think God's heart feels when you ignore Him?

_____

_____

_____

_____

4. Why do you think God wants to spend time with you on a daily basis?

_____

_____

_____

5. Name 3 things you can do to start having a better relationship with Jesus.

_____

_____

_____

6. Why is it important to meditate on God's Word?

_____

_____

_____

What About Me?

1. If I could rate my relationship with Christ on a scale of 1-10 (10 being perfect and 1 being the worst), how would I score?

   1 2 3 4 5 6 7 8 9 10

2. Am I willing to take the challenge to read God's Word every day?

   Yes   No

3. How strong is my desire to spend time with God? (10 being the strongest and 1 being the weakest).

   1 2 3 4 5 6 7 8 9 10

4. Do I thank the Lord daily for all that He has done for me? Why or why not?

   _____

   _____

5. Why am I willing or not willing to share my faith with those who need Jesus?

   _____

   _____

6. I would like to do better in the following areas of my spiritual life:

   _____

   _____

   _____

7. Who do I know that is lost and needs me to share the love of Christ with them? (List their names below. Keep this list in an easy to see place and remember their names in prayer on a regular basis.)

   _____

   _____

   _____

8. What are some easy ways I can share my faith with others?

   _____

   _____

   _____

Chapter 3

∽ ∾

She should <u>know</u> that
her body belongs to God
and she should strive to be
pleasing on the inside,
as well as on the outside.

∽ ∾

"What? <u>Know</u> ye not that your body is the temple of the Holy Ghost which is in you, which ye have of God, and you are not your own?" ~ 1 Corinthians 6:19 (KJV)

God's Temple

According to 1 Corinthians 6:19, your body is the temple where the Lord lives! There's a proper balance we need to find when taking care of our outward body, but still not losing our focus on what is in the heart. We'll discuss both topics in this chapter, but first let's look at eight ways to keep our outward appearance in "tiptop" shape! ☺

1. Maintain a Healthy Diet

"You are what you eat." How often have you heard those words? Just think of how you would feel if you were known as a greasy burger and fries. Yuck! I don't know about you, but I would rather be known as something else... almost anything else! ☺ We should put healthy foods into our bodies, not foods that would harm us. And believe me, there are *plenty* of foods that can be harmful!

Now at this point, let me say that what I'll be sharing with you in the next couple pages may seem useless, boring, and even very...adult-like. Yes! I'm sure as far back as the days of Adam and Eve mothers have been reminding their  children *"eat your green vegetables!"* ☺ Well girls, I just so happen to *agree* with your mother that you should indeed eat your green vegetables...and I'm not afraid to admit it! Before you string me up to nearest tree for being a traitor to young people all across the world, let me ask you to just hear me out.

You will only be young once. I repeat: you will only be young *once!* What you put into your body *will* affect you the older you get! That is why you must start taking care of your body while you are still young. No doubt you've heard this thought from adults at some point in your life! As much as you may want to ignore what adults tell you about this, the fact still remains that they have definitely lived longer than you and know a good deal more about life than you do. That makes them experts in their field! So...listen to the experts! ☺

Proper diet and good health can be an area of much debate these days, so I am not making any claims to know it all or have all the answers! That's why every girl should study these things for herself! No one can take care of your body like *you* can.

Living in this world of convenience and drive through windows, it sometimes can be hard to live healthy and make right decisions! In the Bible we read about how Daniel went against the crowd when it came to putting harmful things in his body, and God blessed him for it! ☺ In the first chapter of the book of Daniel, it talks about the diet he and his friends decided to eat instead of the finer delicacies the king offered them. Much to the amazement of the royal officials and everyone else around, Daniel and his friends grew stronger and healthier than all the other young men of the kingdom! The Lord blessed them for obeying, even though it was hard and no one else was doing it!

So! Let's take a look at the foods your body has digested in the last 24 hours... ☺

What You Have Eaten Today	
Breakfast	
Lunch	
Dinner	
Snacks	

As much as possible, we should try to avoid filling our daily diets with certain types of foods that are harmful to our bodies and over-all health. Of course there will always be exceptions, but our bodies will be so much happier if we try to stay away from consuming foods that are *processed, refined and filled with sugar (like fast food or junk food).* So then, let's take a look at things you *should* put into your bodies! ☺

Fresh Fruits	Fresh, raw fruit is much healthier for you than steamed, dried, or canned fruit. When you crave something sweet, instead of snagging a candy bar or doughnut, try some fresh fruit! You have lots to choose from: bananas, peaches, pears, apples, oranges, strawberries, pineapples, and so many more! You might be surprised how refreshingly addictive fresh fruit can become once you give it a chance. Plus, it's *so* good for you! ☺
Fresh Veggies	I discovered my love for fresh green salads about the same time I discovered my inner cravings for green peppers and cucumbers! Weird, I know. (What can I say? I'm a nut! ☺) Getting plenty of fiber in your daily diet is vitally important for your body to function properly. You can find a wonderful source for your fiber in fresh vegetables. Don't just try green veggies, but orange, red and yellow veggies, too. Go ahead and be brave! Try new things! Let's not judge a vegetable by its outward appearance. You might just be surprised. ☺
Grains, Meats, & Dairy	Breads made with whole-wheat are much better for you than those made with white flour. White flour has been bleached, stripping it of its healthy nutrients. Also, typical breakfast cereals are fine in a pinch, but you might try getting more fiber in your diet by eating a bowl of oats in the morning instead. It's also important to have healthy amounts of protein in your diet. Most people find their protein in meats, such as: beef, poultry, or fish. But did you know that nuts and cheeses are also proteins? That's right. Find a good blend of grains, meats, and dairy and you should be on the right track with your diet. ☺
Plenty of Pure Water	Did you know that soda pop actually sucks the Calcium right out of your bones? That's right! Drinking pop also *dehydrates* a person's body. It shocked me to discover that most people live their lives dehydrated as a direct result of not drinking enough water! Since the human body is mostly made up of water it stands to reason that we need a lot of it to keep our bodies functioning properly! Just how much water should you drink a day? LOTS! ☺ To give you a rough estimate, try this: take your body weight and divide by two. This is how many ounces you should drink a day. For example, a girl who weighs 100 pounds should drink at least 50 ounces of water a day. It's really not that much once you get in the habit. So don't wait! Grab that water bottle and start drinking. ☺

Keep in mind that this diet discussion is only *one* tiny aspect of healthy living. I hope you'll take what we learn here and study nutrition for yourself. We shouldn't just assume this kind of thing is for people like our parents to be concerned about! Because believe me...there's no better time than the present to begin taking *good care* of your body – God's Temple. ☺

2. Exercise Regularly

God designed our bodies to need exercise. I can't even list all the great benefits to remaining physically active because there are so many! ☺ We should *all* have a regular workout routine to help keep our bodies fit and strong.

Realize that you don't *have* to do a massive workout routine that takes hours every day of your life. If you are consistent with a set amount of regular exercises, then that's enough! Eventually you may want to work up to more, but that's up to you whenever you're ready. ☺

Below is a chart for you to keep track of your weekly workout. Write down how many repetitions you do of each activity.

ACTIVITY	*Monday*	*Tuesday*	*Wednesday*	*Thursday*	*Friday*	*Saturday*
Sit Ups						
Push Ups						
Jumping Jacks						
Leg Extensions						
Bicycling (in minutes)						
Other						

Now I have to be honest and let you know that sometimes it's downright *hard* for me to remain focused and faithful with my daily workout routine! And it's not that I dislike working out or anything like that. It's simply that I lack a little thing called *motivation.*

I know you girls have experienced lack of motivation at some point or another as well (whether you will admit it or not ☺)!! When this feeling begins to creep into our bodies, we simply *have* to fight it. We must fight that urge to grab a bag of potato chips and lay around like a bum all day! Listen to the words of Apostle Paul in 1 Corinthians 9:24-27 (NLT):

> *"Remember that in a race everyone runs, but only one person gets the prize.*
> *You also must run in such a way that you will win. All athletes practice strict self-control.*
> *They do it to win a prize that will fade away, but we do it for an eternal prize. So I run*
> *straight to the goal with purpose in every step. I am not like a boxer who misses his punches.*
> *I discipline my body like an athlete, training it to do what it should. Otherwise, I fear that*
> *after preaching to others I myself might be disqualified."*

Did you hear what Paul said? He said he runs *straight* to the goal with purpose in *every step.* Wouldn't it be great if we could be like this when we are tempted to give up or quit?? We shouldn't allow our feelings to dictate whether or not we will be faithful with what we need to do. Let's never give up! May we press on even when things get tough! It's my prayer that we will *all* practice self-control on a daily basis and not only make the easy, soft choices in life. Just remember girls, God gave us these bodies and we need to take care of them. ☺

A Few Exercising Suggestions:

Do something physical every day!

Run, jog, walk, bicycle, swim, or become involved in some kind of organized sport.

Find a buddy to workout with and keep yourself accountable!

To avoid muscle strains or cramps, stretch before and after you work out.

When your body is tired, work your mind. When your mind is tired, work your body!

3. Maintain Proper Posture

The way we walk, stand or sit can reveal a lot about us. Bad posture can reveal bad attitudes. So, hold yourself tall. Stand erect with your shoulders rolled back! When you sit down, sit with your back straight (but not rigid) on the very edge of your seat. Then slowly ease back into the chair. (And remember not to sprawl your legs out when you sit down! ☺)

Posture Check List

- ❑ *Do you hold your head & neck upright?*

- ❑ *Is your back straight?*

- ❑ *Do you slump when you sit?*

- ❑ *Are your legs together?*

When I was younger, I thought that slouching my shoulders and hanging my head was okay because I wasn't trying to draw attention to myself. (After all, I didn't want to seem prideful or arrogant now, did I? ☺) Well, I discovered that having bad posture actually drew a lot of attention to myself! Without realizing it, hanging my head and slumping my shoulders gave a silent message to others that I was insecure and unhappy with the way the Lord made me. That's why I'm glad to hold my body erect with strength and dignity now! It's a way of giving God glory! It also lets others know that I'm happy with the way Jesus made me. *Why don't* **you** *give it a try?* ☺

4. Choose Proper Clothing

1. Be clean & tidy

    - Make sure your clothes are ironed and that they fit properly.

    - When it's possible, tuck your shirt in nicely and neatly.

    - If your shirtsleeves are too long, roll them up.

    - Polish your shoes regularly to remove any scuffs or scratches.

    > *"Your clothes speak even before you do."*
    > *~ Jacqueline Murray*

2. Choose clothes that won't go out of style in the next few weeks.

    - There's nothing wrong with looking "in style". We should try not to be the first one to chase after the latest fads! ☺

    - Remember that people are always watching to see what you will do, what you will wear, and what you will say. Let's set *good* examples!

    - We tell a lot about ourselves by the clothing we choose to wear. We should also endeavor to be a good example to those little eyes that are watching. Most importantly, we should always try to please God by what we wear.

3. Dress Modestly

    - Just remember to avoid anything too tight, too low, too short, or too big. These things will be a cause for distraction (not to mention they are often uncomfortable to wear!). But don't worry...we will discuss this and how it relates to guys in more detail in chapter six! ☺

    - Be sure to listen to your parents when it comes to clothing. They've been at this a lot longer than you have and they could have some great suggestions if you are willing to listen. Really!

4. Dress appropriately for the occasion.

    - Obviously, don't wear overalls to a homecoming dance or a ball gown to the Super Bowl! Use common sense, and when in doubt, call a friend and ask her what *she* is going to wear. That way, if you're wrong you won't be the only one dressed a certain way. (Believe me, this will save you much embarrassment!)

For those of you who'd like to have a few more hints on what to wear and when to wear it, I've listed some possible guidelines below. Keep in mind, these are just some *basic* guidelines you may like to follow. Ultimately what a girl wears is based upon what she owns, where she is going, what she is comfortable in, and what her authorities (God, mom and dad, etc.) would like her to wear! ☺

DRESS CLOTHES	Appropriate for fancy restaurants, ceremonies, church services, weddings, funerals, and receptions. For young ladies such as ourselves, dress clothes could include several of the following: ✓ *Skirt or Dress* ✓ *Nice Blouse (sorry, no T-shirts! ☺)* ✓ *Hose (no socks)* ✓ *Dress Shoes (no sneakers, or flip flops)* ✓ *Nice Pants Suit (worn with hose and dress shoes)*
DRESSY CASUAL CLOTHES	Appropriate for slightly less formal social gatherings, such as baby showers, birthday parties, and so on. For occasions like these, you might try a combination of the following: ✓ *Shirt with a collar, or nice T-Shirt* ✓ *Dress Pants (khaki is a nice dress down option)* ✓ *Semi-Casual Skirt (khaki or denim are acceptable)* ✓ *Leather Shoes or nice Sandals*
CAUSAL CLOTHES	Appropriate for a picnic or a ball game type setting. Many varieties of casual clothes can be worn here: ✓ *T-Shirt* ✓ *Jeans, Overalls, or Khaki Pants* ✓ *Comfortable Skirt* ✓ *Nice Shorts (no cut-offs)* ✓ *Tennis Shoes, Sandals, or Flip Flops* ✓ *Socks*
PLAY CLOTHES	Appropriate for games or work related activities. These clothes need to be comfortable for being very active, having fun, getting dirty, or all three! ☺ ✓ *Old T-Shirt* ✓ *Worn Jeans, Sweat Pants, or Sweat suit* ✓ *Shorts* ✓ *Sneakers*

TIME TO THINK!

1. **Read Daniel Chapter 1. How did the diet Daniel and his friends choose to eat honor God?**

_____

_____

_____

2. **Name a few types of food that you should avoid as much as possible:**

_____

_____

_____

3. **Why is it important to drink plenty of water on a daily basis?**

_____

_____

4. **Maintaining physical activity is not that big of a deal.   True   False**
   Explain your answer:

_____

_____

_____

5. **How can a girl's posture reveal her attitude to others?**

_____

_____

_____

6. **Circle the appropriate place you would wear ratty jeans and an old T-shirt:**

   a) **A wedding shower**
   b) **Outside doing yard work**
   c) **At a fancy restaurant**

What About Me?

1. How is my over all health?

   GOOD   FAIR   POOR

2. My diet is:

ALWAYS GREAT   MOSTLY FINE   NOT GOOD OR BAD   IN NEED OF WORK

3. I'd like to make improvement with my diet in these ways:

_____

_____

4. My exercise is:

ALWAYS GREAT   MOSTLY FINE   NOT GOOD OR BAD   IN NEED OF WORK

5. I'd like to make improvement with my exercise in these ways:

_____

_____

6. My posture is:

ALWAYS GREAT   MOSTLY FINE   NOT GOOD OR BAD   IN NEED OF WORK

7. I'd like to make improvement with my posture in these ways:

_____

_____

8. My choice in clothing is:

ALWAYS GREAT   MOSTLY FINE   NOT GOOD OR BAD   IN NEED OF WORK

9. I'd like to make improvement with my clothing in these ways:

_____

5. Maintain Proper Skin Care

Beauty is *not* skin deep! I know that's contrary to what the world is constantly telling us today. Really though, having a beautiful outward appearance should *not* be our main focus. It should *always* be on what's in our hearts. However, even though the focus is on our hearts, we still need to be attentive to our outward appearance as well! ☺

Now, the type of skin care products you use is up to you. For myself (in an effort to be as healthy as possible ☺), I've tried to use all-natural skin care products. My skin has absolutely *loved* using products that contain organic compounds rather than man-made chemicals! ☺ So that's just something to think about the next time you go to the store on a search for that perfect new skin care product.

Basic Skin Care Steps

1. **Wash** – Wet your face with warm water.
2. **Cleanse** – Gently rub cleanser in with a warm washcloth.
3. **Moisturize** – Pat face dry. Use plenty of lotion or oil on your face and neck.

Dry Skin:	Pimply Skin	Oily Skin:
Find a lotion or oil especially made for dryness. You can also use a washcloth to gently rub away dead skin. Sometimes facial masks are good for dry skin, too. The key to dry skin is to *moisturize.*	Avoid touching your pimples too often, and be sure to wash your face at least twice a day. Don't use rough rags on your face, or facial scrubs with granules in them that may cause irritation. The most important thing to do with pimples is keep smiling! ☺	Oily skinned people need to stay away from extra moisturizing creams. Oil-free lotions are best. Alcohol on a cotton ball helps remove oil. Sometimes a good facial powder will take away that greasy look.

6. Consider Makeup Wisely

Whether or not a girl should wear makeup (and when she should begin wearing it) is between the girl, God, and her parents. Makeup is merely a tool. It's our attitude and motivation behind using this tool that matters. I personally feel that there is nothing wrong with using makeup for the sake of enhancing your features, but if you apply too much makeup (or apply it improperly) you will just draw attention to yourself. You may be thinking to yourself, "Why is that so bad? I like attention!" The Scriptures tell us in Philippians 2:3 that we should "Do nothing out of selfish ambition or vain conceit, but in humility consider others better than yourselves." (NIV) Can you honestly say that when you want others to look at you, you are avoiding selfishness and considering others better than yourself? Yikes! That's convicting for me! ☺

> *"A beautiful soul shining out of a plain face is far more attractive than a beautiful face out of which looks a soul full of selfishness and coldness."*
> *~ Karen Andreola*

Some girls wear makeup to "make themselves beautiful", but I think that's terribly sad. ☹ That reason alone should *never* be why a girl wears makeup. This outward appearance will only fade away! Our hearts are what we should strive to always keep beautiful, and the only way we can do that is through *Jesus Christ*.

Now it's Myklin's confession time! <sigh> I *love* makeup. I read books about it, I talk about it, I watch how other people wear it, blah, blah, blah. So of course, I could spend pages and pages talking about it! I like how extremely versatile makeup is. There's a lot that can be said about it, but I will do my best to just hit the highlights and keep this simple.

I often have to remind myself that makeup is not the key to being beautiful. I should never look in the mirror after applying my makeup and think, "Okay, *now* I like myself." I should be content with the way God has designed me and yet still strive to look my best on the outside, too. *Balance* is the key! God loves inward beauty, so if that is my focus then *He* will honored. ☺

My parents didn't let me wear full makeup until I turned sixteen, so I had a lot of anticipation behind the whole makeup thing when I finally got to wear it! I had read all the books, studied the techniques, and knew exactly what I was going to do. However, it took me a lot of trial and error before I found a look that was right for me.

So with that said, I realize we are all at different stages of life. Maybe you're not ready to consider wearing makeup, or maybe you've been wearing it for years! I don't know. ☺ That's why we will just discuss the basics here. Feel free to skip this section if you think makeup isn't for you. The reason we will spend time on this subject is simply because so many girls jump right into wearing makeup and become confused as to the best way to do it.

Remember, makeup is to enhance your features, not to "make" you beautiful! ☺

So...without any further adieu, let's get started! ☺

1. FOUNDATION	Make sure you have found the right shade that matches your current skin tone (your skin tone will most likely change with the seasons! ☺). Apply with your fingertip or a sponge. Dot foundation over the central part of your face, including your eyelids. Blend well (especially around your jaw and hair line).	**HINTS** You might want to add a little extra foundation to areas on your face where you may have blemishes, redness, or dark circles. Watch out for blotches of foundation in concentrated areas. You may try getting the tip of your finger wet and gently evening out the foundation when this happens.
2. FACIAL POWDER	As with foundation, find a facial powder that is consistent with the tone of your skin. Dust a light layer of powder over your face (including your eyelids) with either a powder puff or a makeup brush.	**HINTS** Compact powder is a little firmer than regular powder and would be a good choice to carry in your purse or when traveling. Be sure to avoid "over-powdering." ☺
3. EYE BROWS	Use tweezers to thin your eyebrows a little bit, making sure to remove the extra hair between your eyebrows along the bridge of your nose. Follow the natural growth as much as possible.	**HINTS** Be careful not to over-tweeze! If you do happen to get tweezer happy, find an eyebrow pencil the color of your eyebrows and gently fill in the "holes" where you have over-tweezed. ☺

41

4. EYE COLOR

You may like to try several coordinating colors of eye makeup. However, pick them carefully! Look for colors that compliment your eyes, making sure they do not distract or draw too much attention. Apply lightly at first. Blend well.

HINTS

There are many different techniques to apply color to your eyes and many involve a great deal of time to achieve. You should find a look that is simple, but still nice. I would definitely suggest trying lighter, more neutral colors for everyday wear! ☺

5. EYE LINER

Eyeliner is specifically designed for definition. Using an eye pencil, draw a line as close to your lashes as you can get. Make sure you blend very well so that it doesn't look like you drew it on with a Magic Marker®! ☺

HINTS

You should match the width of the line you draw to the size of your eyelids. If you have large eyelids, you should apply a wider line; or if you have small eyelids, apply a thin line.

6. MASCARA

Like eyeliner, mascara is designed for definition. It defines your eyelashes. Mascara comes in all different styles and colors (so that means you can have a lot of fun finding what you like)! Brush on mascara with gentle strokes. Smooth out clumps with lash separator.

HINTS

If your lashes are short, look for a good lengthening mascara. If they are thin, use thickening mascara. Brown mascara works nicely for a more natural look.

7. BLUSH	Choose a soft shade to begin with. Apply directly under your cheekbones. Blend well.	**HINTS** Be sure not to apply the blush too high on your temples or cheekbones. Also, avoid applying the blush on the center of your cheeks. ☺

8. LIPSTICK	Wear lipstick with discretion (if you choose to wear it at all). Be sure not to overdo your lipstick like so many girls do. Find a shade that does *not* distract from the rest of your appearance! Let's not simply see your big *red lips* and completely miss the beautiful smile behind it. ☺	**HINTS** To avoid excessive dryness, moisturize lips often. Glosses can also have a nice effect for either dressy or causal occasions! ☺

A Few Makeup Suggestions:

Avoid bright blue eye shadow.
It was highly over-rated (and over-used!) in the 60s and 70s and is now considered bad taste.

Don't worry about smudges or mistakes! Cotton swabs take care of touch ups, but when it's a big mistake, it may be best to just start over. ☺

Be sure to remove all your makeup at the end of the day!
A little bit of baby oil on a cotton ball works well.

When it comes to makeup, more is not necessarily better! It's just… more. ☺

*Never use makeup because you dislike the way you have been made. God made you beautiful just the way you are! Be sure you are content with your looks **before** you start experimenting with makeup.*

Don't be afraid to show your face without any makeup on whatsoever! ☺

7. Remember Your Nails

When I shake hands with a girl who has fingernails that are clean and clipped, it tells me that she is caring for some of the small details of her outward appearance. Unkempt nails give a girl the look of sloppiness. We don't want the little things of our outward appearance to become our focus, but let's not forget them either! ☺

Basic Nail Care:

- *Clean hands and nails with warm soap and water.*

- *Use a brush to scrub under nails and to remove any imbedded dirt.*

- *Use clippers to trim nails regularly (no biting! ☺).*

- *Use lotion to keep skin and hands moisturized.*

A More Manicured Look:

- *Shape nails with an emery board.*

- *Push cuticles back gently with a cuticle stick.*

- *Remove any hangnails with clippers.*

- *Apply fingernail polish if desired. (When choosing colors, remember that neutral colors will go with more outfits!)*

TIME TO THINK!

1. A girl should always strive to be beautiful on the outside first and then work on the inside.

   True   False

2. An oily skinned girl should use the most moisturizing lotion she can find.

   True   False

3. What kind of facial powder is good for carrying in your purse or for taking on road trips?

---

4. A girl should never tweeze between her eyebrows on the brim of her nose. The uni-brow look is *in!*

   True   False

5. The proper place a girl should apply blush is:

   a.)   Directly under cheekbones
   b.)   In the very center of her cheeks
   c.)   On her temples

6. A girl should wear the same color of foundation year round.

   True   False

7. What kind of mascara is good for a natural look?

   a.)   Black Mascara
   b.)   Blue Mascara
   c.)   Lengthening Mascara
   d.)   Brown Mascara

8. It is acceptable to occasionally trim your nails by biting.

   True   False

What About Me?

1. Do I think that a girl's attractiveness comes solely from the inside or the outside? Why or why not?

_____

_____

2. Who do I try to please when it comes to my outward appearance?

_____

3. Am I quick to judge others by their outward appearance? Why or why not?

_____

_____

_____

4. What are my feelings about wearing makeup?

_____

_____

_____

5. If I currently wear makeup, what is the motivation of my heart for doing so?

_____

_____

_____

6. Write 1 Samuel 16:7 on the lines below:

_____

_____

_____

7. What does this verse mean to me in regards to wearing makeup?

_____

_____

_____

8. Maintain Proper Hair Care

It is always important to take some time to properly fix your hair before you start the day. However, there are so many varieties of styles, textures and colors of hair, that it often makes finding the look that is completely *you* difficult! I know how it is to try out tons of different things and end up not really being happy with any of them! Sometimes it takes a while to find what is exactly right for you. Here are some steps we should take before we actually start on that search for the perfect look...

BASIC HAIR CARE:

✓ BRUSH DAILY—Start with the ends of your hair and work up. Be sure not to over brush *or* under brush your hair... ☺

✓ CLEANSE OFTEN—First, wet your hair completely, rub in a small amount of shampoo until lathered, and rinse with water. Rub the same amount of conditioner into your hair and then rinse again.

✓ STYLE—Apply mousse, styling gel or molding spray while your hair is still wet. After your hair is dry (either by air drying or using a hair dryer), curl, comb, brush or twist to achieve your desired style. Touch up with hair spray (but not too much, or you might die from toxic fume inhalation! ☺).

47

1. *Straight Hair*	Pro	↑	Has a beautiful shine. ☺
	Con	↓	Hard to curl... ☹
	Pro	↑	All one consistency and thickness. ☺
	Con	↓	Often very heavy... ☹
2. *Wavy Hair*	Pro	↑	Easier to curl than straight hair. ☺
	Con	↓	Can look disheveled... ☹
	Pro	↑	Can have nice thickness and pliability. ☺
	Con	↓	Not very many people have it... ☹
3. *Curly Hair*	Pro	↑	People with straight hair want it. ☺
	Con	↓	Very high maintenance... ☹
	Pro	↑	Can achieve versatility with ease. ☺
	Con	↓	Heat sensitive, dry, and frizzy... ☹
4. *Kinky Hair*	Pro	↑	Benefits from conditioning. ☺
	Con	↓	Most fragile type of hair... ☹
	Pro	↑	Relaxes, holds style and straightens easily. ☺
	Con	↓	Frizzy and traps oil in the scalp... ☹

Most people have a mixture of these different types of hair. (I certainly do!) The main thing is to learn how to do the best with whatever type of hair you have. Here are a few ideas listed below... ☺

- Dry Hair

Try conditioning your hair more than once. (Completely rinse out the conditioner before applying any more.) Be very careful not to over brush your hair. This will only make your hair more dry.

- Oily Hair

Shampooing your hair twice will help take out some of the oil. Make sure you wash your hair *every* day to keep that "greasy" look from popping up. (No one likes that look anyway! ☺)

- Extra Thin Hair

You might try what is known as back-combing (or teasing). This is done by combing back and forth underneath a select portion of your hair, then gently brushing over the area. This will give a little added *lift* to your normally flat hair! Or flip your head over and brush your hair just like you normally would, except from the underneath side. Sometimes this helps to give your hair some more bounce! ☺ You also may want to find a shampoo and conditioner made especially for adding volume to your hair.

- Frizzy Hair

Sometimes blow-drying frizzy hair only makes it worse. I'd suggest letting your hair air dry for a change and see if that helps at all. To care for the inevitable fly away look that comes with frizzy hair, you may try putting smoothing gel or some lotion on your hands and gently running it through your hair. And remember, a little bit goes a long way. Straightening tongs or a jumbo-sized curling iron can help take away the frizz that may be bothering you. See what works best for you! ☺

How do you know what hairstyle is best for you?

Before you can find what style is best for you, you must first determine what kind of facial shape you have. Here are five different types of face shapes...

Oval

The oval is often considered the easiest facial shape to work with. Depending on how strong the person's facial features are they may try layering around the face to give some dimension to it. Bangs can be a nice way to offset the look of an intensely oval face! ☺

Heart

This is also known as triangular. An easy cut to compliment this facial shape is an inverted triangle. Curly or wavy hairstyles are often nice for a softening effect to the severe appearance of a triangular face. Stay away from cuts that are too heavy on top. ☺

Square

This facial shape can give someone a look of strength (especially with a very pronounced jaw line). Layers around the face, as well as curly or wavy hairstyles, will soften a harsh looking facial structure. ☺ *The length of the cut should extend past the jaw line. Avoid flat or pulled back styles.*

Long

This face can be easily exaggerated, but with the proper style, the effect can be rather striking! ☺ *Focusing layers around the face will help with definition. Avoid long, one length, or "top heavy" hairstyles. A part that is on the side of the head, rather than down the middle, will give the illusion of more roundness.*

Round

Those with round faces often have less defined features. Avoid curly or wavy styles that add width to the sides and only accentuate the roundness of this face. However, subtle layers around the face, added fullness to the top of the hair, or one-length cuts, will help to frame this facial shape. ☺

Styling Techniques . . .

Rollers

❖ Tiny ringlets—Use SMALL ROLLERS

❖ Gentle waves—Use MEDIUM ROLLERS

❖ Softly curled ends—Use LARGE ROLLERS

❖ Body and fullness—Use JUMBO ROLLERS

Tips

Don't bunch a section of hair in the middle of the rollers. For lasting curls, apply a little bit of hairspray or gel to each section before winding it. Use a pick to gently comb out curls.

Curling Irons

❖ Great for last minute touch ups.

❖ Use a medium size iron to curl ends out or under.

❖ For wisps of hair and tendrils, try a small iron.

Tips

Be careful not to burn yourself! Seriously, girls…take it from the queen of curling iron burns! ☺ Begin cautiously at first. Experiment with different sizes of irons for different curl styles.

Hair Dryers

❖ Keep dryer 3-6 inches away from hair.

❖ Dry hair with head upright and gently run fingers through strands (starting at the roots). This gives a more natural look.

❖ For fullness, flip head over and dry from underneath.

❖ Use a brush to roll hair, giving it a styled look.

Tips

To keep from scorching your hair, avoid drying in more than one spot for too long. Try a cool setting if your hair is not completely wet to begin with. Running over your hair with a dryer at the end of the day will help give it some life. ☺

The different hairstyles available to you are limitless!! Some people pick one style and stick with it the rest of their lives. Generally, it's a good idea to gradually shorten your hair the older you get. However, I know lots of young women with short hair and older women with long hair! It's all up to you. Your hairstyle can reflect your mood or personality. Just remember to keep it simple!

A fancier hairstyle is perfectly acceptable for a special occasion such as a wedding or award ceremony. A ball game or picnic is definitely the appropriate time to wear a headband or ponytail. What can I say? Just have fun with your hair. ☺

> *"Your beauty should not come from outward adornment, such as braided hair and the wearing of gold jewelry and fine clothes. Instead, it should be that of your inner self, the unfading beauty of a gentle and quiet spirit, which is of great worth in God's sight. For this is the way the holy women of the past who put their hope in God used to make themselves beautiful..."* ~ 1 Peter 3:3-5 (NIV)

A Few Hair Suggestions:

Trim your hair regularly.

Don't over brush.

Every now and then try a new shampoo or conditioner.

Clean your brushes, combs and curling irons often.

Pay attention to other people's hair and copy the things you like.

Remember to work with the shape of your face, not against it.

Be sure to thank God for whatever type of face & hair you have!

Never forget... He DOESN'T make mistakes!

TIME TO THINK!

1. Should a girl be overly concerned with her hair?   Yes   No

2. Should a girl be unconcerned with her hair?   Yes   No

3. A girl should choose the most elaborate and stylish hairdo she can find.

    True   False

4. Kinky hair can benefit from a good conditioner.

    True   False

5. Girls with long faces should wear their hair straight, long and all one length.

    True   False

6. Describe two ways a girl can put more fullness into her hair:

_____

_____

7. What are a few of the characteristics of someone with a square face?

_____

_____

8. How far away from her hair should a girl hold her hair dryer?

    a. 5 - 6 inches
    b. 1 – 2 inches
    c. 8 – 10 inches
    d. 3 – 6 inches

What kind of hairstyle is good for me?

1. My type of hair: _____

2. My facial shape: _____

3. My lifestyle (laid back, busy, etc.): _____

4. Does my schedule allow for a more involved hair routine?   Yes   No

5. Am I in need of a change in my hairstyle?   Yes   No

6. Do I want a cute, pretty, simple, or dramatic look?

   _____

   _____

7. How can I go about achieving this look?

   _____

   _____

   _____

8. What are some ways I can maintain a healthy balance in taking the time to properly fix my hair without becoming too absorbed with absolute perfection?

   _____

   _____

   _____

Remember...your outward appearance is important because if you have Jesus in your heart, your body is the temple of the Holy Spirit! So...don't you think you should treat it that way?? ☺

Chapter 4

ॐ ॐ

She should <u>know</u> how
to look for good character in
the people she chooses to
spend time with and treat
as role models.

ॐ ॐ

"...<u>know</u> ye not that the friendship of the world is enmity with God?"
~ James 4:4b (KJV)

ഇ ൙

True Friendships

   Whether we realize it or not, we are influenced by the people around us. Peer pressure comes into play nearly every day of our lives! That's why it is important to choose friends who won't lead us into the wrong things.

> "He that walketh with wise men shall be wise: but a companion of fools shall be destroyed."
> ~ Proverbs 13:20 (KJV)

   We have talked about this before and I will say it again...people are *always* watching us! Our parents are watching, our friends are watching, strangers are watching, but most importantly, *God* is always watching. ☺ I don't know about you, but that convicts me. I want Him to be pleased with those I choose to spend time with and call my friends! *Don't you?* ☺

> "A true friend is one who knows you as you really are, understands where you've been, accepts who you've become, and still gently invites you to grow."
> ~ Unknown

57

Become a True Friend

> *"But the fruit of the Spirit is love, joy, peace, patience, kindness, goodness, faithfulness, gentleness and self-control. Against such things there is no law."*
> ~ *Galatians 5:22-23 (NIV)*

- Be a friend to the friendless. (Luke 6:32-36)

- Don't return hurt for hurt. (Matthew 5:38-44)

- Be honest and truthful, but share that truth in love. ☺ (Ephesians 4:15)

- Don't put an age limit on your friendships.

- Have a kind word and a smile ready to give at a moment's notice. ☺

- Do your best not to take up an offense. (1 Thessalonians 5:15)

- Avoid being involved in cliques that may pressure you not to get to know other people.

- Ask the Lord to help you be friendly to those people who are hard to get to know.

- Remember, a person is made better or worse by friends. Don't you want to be the kind of friend that makes others better? ☺

> *"A man that hath friends must show himself friendly: and there is a friend that sticketh closer than a brother."* ~ *Proverbs 18:24 (KJV)*

Or in the words of my mother, *"Myklin, if you want to have friends, you must first BE a friend."*

TIME TO THINK!

1. Have you ever been on the outside of a group of friends? What did it feel like?

_____

_____

_____

2. Have you ever been involved with a group of friends who excluded other people?

_____

_____

3. How does God feel about friends who pressure you to ignore others?

_____

_____

_____

4. What are some ways you can involve other people into your group of friends?

_____

_____

_____

5. What do you think it means to "not take up an offense"?

_____

_____

6. Are you the kind of friend who makes other people better? If not, how can you become this sort of friend?

_____

_____

_____

What About Me?

1. How do I treat people who are hard to get along with?

_____

_____

2. Why is it hard for me to get along with some people?

_____

_____

_____

3. I need to become better friends with these people:

_____

_____

_____

4. What are some easy ways that I can start right now to become that better friend?

_____

_____

_____

5. Is Jesus happy with my choice of friends? Why or why not?

_____

_____

6. Why is it important to choose my friends wisely?

_____

_____

7. What does it mean to be a "companion of fools"? (Proverbs 13:20)

_____

_____

_____

Demonstrate Good Manners

Have you ever stopped to take notice of how most young people conduct themselves when they are out in public? It's sad what you see. ☹ Teenagers and pre-teens are often known for their loud, reckless, and irresponsible behavior. At first I was a little surprised that people would think that about youth in general, until I started paying more attention.

Young folks really *do* act that way! Sadly, it's no wonder people have such low opinions of them. ☹ I'm often devastated to see the example that teens set for those around them. And believe me, I'm not perfect when it comes to this either! Let's face it...sometimes it's hard not to get caught up in the moment and let a few loud or irresponsible things slip from our mouths. After all, we're just having fun...right?

It doesn't have to be that way! Let's not fit into the mold of every other young person in the world today! We can change perspectives by being young people that set good examples in this world. We *can* make a difference by choosing to do what's right, even when no one else is willing to make that sacrifice. ☺ Use *positive* peer pressure to help others decide to do the right thing. It's certainly possible to be a polite and kind young person these days! You just have to *do it!*

Standards are distastefully low when it comes to manners in our society today! ☹ Rarely do we see polite individuals who are willing to go out of their way to do a good deed or two. That reason alone should be enough to make us desire to be kind, decent, and polite. More importantly, the Bible is full of principles about loving others, showing kindness to those in need, and demonstrating respect to one's authorities. We all need to know what good manners are and how to use them correctly!

The Bible has this to say on the matter...

> *"Do to others as you would have them do to you."* ~ Luke 6:31 (NIV)
>
> *"[Love] is not rude..."* ~ 1 Corinthians 13:5a (NIV)
>
> *"My command is this: Love each other as I have loved you. Greater love has no one than this, that he lay down his life for his friends."* ~ John 15:12-13 (NIV)

When we demonstrate good manners to those around us (friends, family, strangers, etc.), we are really showing them a little bit of the love that Jesus has for us. Some of these things we'll be discussing in this section might be a review for you, but what's wrong with a review? ☺ Now, do you think you are ready for this? I mean, c'mon now...this stuff isn't for the faint of heart! ☺

Meeting New People	
Smile Warmly.	*A smile is worth more than a thousand words! You may be able to fluently spout off the most courteous introductions in the world, but if you have the smile of someone who has been sucking on a sour grapefruit all day, it won't mean a thing! ☺ Don't be afraid to smile. Go ahead. You'll see for yourself how contagious it is. (P.S. This is the **most** important part of introductions!)*
Stand Tall.	*No one likes a "sloucher." Just think about it! Do you know how much it says to the person you are meeting if you hold yourself tall and face them squarely? It says a lot, that's for sure! It says that you respect them enough to give them your full attention - to listen intently to what they have to say.*
Look the person directly in the eyes.	*This shows them that you aren't hiding anything and that you aren't afraid to be honest with them. The Bible warns about those people with "shifty eyes." Truthfulness or deceit can be found by looking into the eyes of a human being. What's in your eyes?*
Give a firm handshake.	*None of this wimpy little girl hand shakin', ladies! Be firm, but not painful in your grip. Again, this is an upfront and mannerly thing to do when meeting someone new. People will greatly appreciate this (especially the older generation)! ☺*
Pay careful attention to their name.	*This is hard to do for most people (myself included)! ☺ Listen to catch the person's name and then repeat it back (making sure you have the correct pronunciation). Hint to the wise: repeating their name back to them is also good for **your** memory. The more times you can say it, the better!*

How to properly introduce someone:

"Katie, I don't think you've met my friend Amber. Katie, this is Amber. Amber, this is Katie."

"Josh, I'd like to introduce my friend, Heather. Heather, this is Josh."

How to properly accept an introduction:

"It is nice to meet you, Sarah." or, "How do you do, Sarah?" or, "My pleasure, Sarah."

Out In Public	
Be courteous and respectful to those you are with, as well as to those you may meet along the way.	*Often we forget common courtesies while we're out in public, such as being careful not to gossip about people, or saying "thank you" to a sales clerk. Let's not fall into this trap while we're out and about!* ☺
Keep your volume down.	*This is true not only with music, but with your voices, as well. Laughter is louder than you may think!* ☺
Use discretion when choosing people to go out in public with you.	*Even though you may not be the one setting the bad example, your friend's behavior is reflected on you as well. So, choose your friends wisely!*
Have a good time, but don't go overboard.	*Be sensitive to when things need to stop. If a situation gets out of hand, be kind, but firm. If your friends won't listen to reason, sometimes you may need to just walk away.*
If you are at a restaurant, be sure to leave a nice tip if the service was good (15-25%). Treat your server with kindness and respect.	*Don't laugh or joke at your server. This can be hurtful and is extremely rude. You should also be aware of how long you stay in a restaurant and occupy your table. Your server has many other tables to wait on, so it is respectful not to dawdle, taking up more of their precious time than is necessary. If you do happen to stay a long time at the table, ask your server if he or she needs your table to seat other people who are waiting to eat. Also, don't forget to leave a generous tip.* ☺

Attending Parties

Come only if invited (RSVP if necessary).	*If you don't want to go or are unable to, let your hostess know with ample time to spare before the party. (P.S. Do so with kindness and respect! ☺)*
Volunteer to bring something, if needed.	*It's always nice to offer to bring something to the party, like a volleyball net, board game, food dish, etc. ☺*
Follow the instructions of the hostess.	*That means if your hostess asks you to come dressed in a purple zebra tutu, then come in the best purple zebra tutu you have (even if it sounds ludicrous and none of the other guests do so)!*
Come promptly and on time!	*This is tough one, I know! As hard as it may be for so many people to arrive on time, it's such an important part of good manners. Of course to pull this off we usually have to plan ahead. Yes, this may mean a little inconvenience, but it's definitely worth it. ☺*
If you're early, offer to help prepare for the party.	*See if you can work in the kitchen or outside. This is a good idea even if you're not early—**Always** look for ways to help! ☺*
Visit with as many people as possible, including your hostess.	*Avoid hanging with a few select people throughout the party. This might seem "clique-ish" and make you appear unapproachable, even if you aren't. Who knows? Maybe you'd miss out on making a great new friend! ☺*
Thank your hostess!	*Share with her how much you enjoyed yourself; that is, if indeed you did! ☺ If you didn't enjoy yourself, thank her warmly anyway. Just try to find something good to say about the time you had.*

Being a Hostess

Greet everyone warmly.	*Make each guest feel at home and as comfortable as possible! ☺ Visit with everyone individually before they leave. They need to know they are a special part of your evening. As the hostess, it is up to you to direct the conversation topics and introduce new people to one another.*
Never make demands of your guests.	*Allow guests to have the final "say" when choosing activities. Be sensitive not to place people in awkward positions. For example, some people are just not athletic (like me! ☺), but they still may want to feel included in the activities, even if they decline a sports type of game. Try your best to find something everyone can agree on. But if not, just get several different games going and be sure to try each game yourself.*
When the party is over, show each guest to the door.	*Thank them for coming!! Remember, they didn't have to come, but they did. ☺*

Table Manners

Allow a gentleman to seat you (if he is inclined on being gentlemanly).	*Of course this would be for special occasions! ☺ In most circumstances, you probably shouldn't stand around waiting for a guy to seat you. Simply follow the procedure of those around you to see what is expected in this situation.*
Immediately start a conversation with the people seated next to you.	*Be aware of those who are nearest you and don't exclude anyone from the conversation. Look for a smooth way to bring everyone into the conversation at hand or choose a new topic.*

Unfold your napkin and place it on your lap.	*Let's not be like our brothers and tie the napkin around our necks or tuck it in our belts!* ☺ *Laps will do the job quite nicely.*
Know what utensil to use.	*Generally, a good rule of thumb is to start with the outer edge of the place setting and work in. If you know what each utensil is (soup spoon, dessert fork, salad fork, etc.), then when each course is served, you will know which one to use. If you don't know what every utensil is, just play it cool and stick with whatever utensil you've started to use. (Most likely no one will even notice!!* ☺*) You also don't want to put your silverware back on the table after you've used it. When your meal is finished, place your utensils on your plate, signifying you are finished (see the picture to the left).*
Take small, but adequate portions.	*Chances are you will be offered a second helping and no one wants to look like a glutton, especially if you can come back for more! Plus, taking small portions is courteous to the rest of the dinner party and leaves plenty for them.*
Don't be the first to start eating.	*A wise suggestion would be to wait for your hostess to start eating. Usually she is the signal to allow the start of the meal. There are circumstances when this does not work, so be patient and see what the situation is before you start consuming your scrumptious meal!* ☺
Take small bites.	*You need to be able to carry on a conversation and eat at the same time — a juggling act, I know!* ☺ *If you aren't able to chew a few times and swallow, then you have taken a bite that's too big. It's embarrassing when you are asked a question and you've just shoveled a load of salad in your mouth, making you chew for a minute before answering!* ☺
Chew with your mouth closed.	*No doubt you've heard this one before! It's always good to serve as a reminder. Also, be sure to never slurp any liquids. That's just plain annoying.* ☺
Tilt bowls away from you slightly to scoop up the last bite or two.	*This avoids spilling the contents of your bowl on your lap by tilting too far towards you. (Take it from Myklin, the Perpetual Spiller!* ☺*)*

Elbows off the table!	*This is the custom unless you're at a picnic or barbeque and fried chicken is on your plate. You'll want to keep your elbows from flying out from your sides like wings. Remember, you're not a B-52 Bomber!* ☺
Lean slightly forward with each bite.	*Try not to slouch over your food like a vulture, but keep an arch in your back and throw your shoulders back. After all, who really wants to watch a vulture hungrily devour its meal?* ☺
Remember to use your napkin.	*The safe thing to do is dab your mouth with your napkin after every bite.* ☺
Don't talk with your hands while holding silverware or food.	*Wouldn't it be simply terrible if you were telling a rather animated story and a clump of Jell-O® went flying from your spoon and hit your Aunt Agatha in the face?? Yes it would! That's why we should avoid excessive hand motions at the table (even though it's sometimes hard to do)!* ☺

Take a small portion of every food you are offered.	*The exception to this would be if you are allergic or have violent reactions to a certain type of food offered you. Never grimace, scowl, or groan when a certain food is tasted that disagrees with you. If you are asked if you like a certain type of food that's distasteful to you, certainly be honest, but also be as polite as possible! Although, it may not be the best thing to tell **everything** you are thinking.* ☺ *It's hard when you're placed in that situation, but just do your best to be polite. Remember to smile often and commend what you **do** enjoy!*

"Gratitude is the most exquisite form of courtesy." ~ Unknown

Do your best to eat everything on your plate.	Sometimes this cannot be done! ☺ You may have a portion that is simply too large for your stomach to handle, or the food may be making your stomach feel like an ocean at high tide! ☺ In such cases, apologize to your hostess for not finishing your food, and thank her for preparing such a nice meal. If you ever feel like you're going to be sick, definitely **remove yourself** from the dinner party and hurry to the nearest restroom! If you can conceal your discomfort from your hostess, it would be nice. However, be honest if the subject comes up.

"Eating slowly helps to keep one slim; in other words, haste makes waist." ~ A. H. Hallock

Be liberal with gratitude to your hostess.	Thank her for the meal, tell her what your favorite part was, and let her know how much you enjoyed yourself. As always, even if you didn't enjoy the meal that much, try to find something positive to say! ☺ Also try to help clean up after the meal. Your hostess may not accept your offer to help, but she should be blessed by it.
When an accident occurs, apologize and then move on. 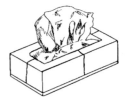	Sometimes things happen that we cannot control. If you burp, excuse yourself and do your best to squelch it the next time! If something is lodged in your tooth, ignore it until the meal is over and then retreat to the bathroom and do your best to remove the pesky piece of food! Excuse yourself from the table if you need to blow your nose, and do so in a way that will not draw attention. Oh, and girls, please blow your nose in a Kleenex®, **not** in a napkin. ☺ If you cough or choke on food, turn your head and cover your mouth with your napkin until your choking or coughing has subsided. Drink water as you are able between coughs. Just focus on breathing and don't worry about what others are thinking of you! You should be cautious to leave the room because of embarrassment since choking is very dangerous.

68

Meaningful Conversations

Know when to speak and when not to speak.	I read the above quote on a church billboard once and it has stuck with me! We should remember Ecclesiastes 3:7b, which says, "...a time to be silent and a time to speak." (NIV) Ask God to show you when to speak and when not to speak! Don't be afraid of silence, yet at the same time you should never dominate the conversation! ☺ We should always strive to have proper balance with both of these two extremes.
Make sure to never interrupt.	I don't know about you, but interruptions happen most often within my family. Unfortunately, I usually think that what I have to say is more important than what one of them is saying, and that results in me jumping in to tell them everything that I am thinking! Proverbs 18:13 says, "He who answers before listening — that is his folly and his shame." (NIV) Avoid this at all costs, ladies! When an interruption does occur, we should quickly apologize and ask the other person to please go on with what they were saying.
Use words full of kindness, respect, gratitude, and understanding.	I learned when I was young to always say, "Please", "Thank you", and "You're welcome". This is one habit worth reviving! We should never be above speaking these words of kindness!! ☺
Never make jokes at the expense of another person.	Be the defender of the weak! Put yourself in their shoes. Never have anything bad to say about another person. When you make a mistake, own up to it, and ask that person to forgive you.
Look for something positive to say.	You can find plenty of positive things to talk about! Why not fill your conversation with discussions of God's greatness, and the wonderful things He has done for you and those around you?? You definitely can't go wrong there! ☺

Try to keep the conversation going.	*You should always be thinking of something else to say or another question to ask. (I think of this as my own personal arsenal of conversation topics!! ☺) When you're trying to focus the conversation on the other person, this shows them that you are truly interested and care about them! They should appreciate this greatly.*
Be other-oriented.	*Who likes a girl who can only speak about herself? This is conceited and completely self-centered. Now, this doesn't mean you can never talk about yourself. Just wait to be prompted. Know when to direct the conversation back to another person and away from yourself! (HINT: Look at the life of Jesus! How often did He talk about Himself? He was always far more genuinely interested in others. We should be the same way!)*
Have discernment to know when a conversation needs to end.	*Here are a few good signs you can be aware of when you're trying to judge when a conversation needs to end:* • *The person seems to have lost interest in the conversation* • *You see that it's becoming harder to find things to discuss* • *Someone else needs to speak to you or to the person you're visiting with* • *There are too many distractions to continue talking comfortably*
Never "cling" to, or follow someone around.	*Has anyone ever done this to you? Then you know how hard it can be for the person who is being clung to! You should always be looking for others to speak with and for opportunities to make new friends. ☺*
If you like something about someone, tell them!	*If you like the way someone is compassionate to those who are hurting, tell them! If you admire the endurance someone has when times are tough, share that with them! And trust me... they'll be glad you did. ☺*

> *"Let your conversation be always full of grace, seasoned with salt, so that you may know how to answer everyone." ~ Colossians 4:6 (NIV)*

Conversation Fillers:	Conversation No No's:
"What have you enjoyed the most about this party?" "You know, you look familiar. Have we met?" "Can you believe the weather for this time of year?!" "I LOVE this sea food. Have you tried it yet?" "What school do you go to?" "What keeps you busy?" "Do you have brothers or sisters?" "What do you want to do when you're out of school?" "Do you like music? What kind?" "Have you lived here all your life?"	"How much money do you make?" "How much do you weigh?" "How old are you?" (...to an adult! ☺) "Boy, you sure are annoying." "What made you decide to wear your hair like *that*?" "You know, they have medicine for allergies as *bad* as yours." "You won't believe the awful thing I heard about Julie the other day!"

"Courtesy is plain, old-fashioned thoughtfulness. What will make the other person more comfortable? Do for him or her what you would want done for you. Nobody is born thoughtful. We must all learn it." ~ Elisabeth Elliot

A Few Mannerly Suggestions:

Manners reflect what is inside!

If you care about other people, it will be evident in the way you treat them.

If you only care about yourself, then those around you will quickly notice and they will find ways to avoid or tease you. Who likes to listen to someone go on and on about themselves?

Try looking for that one lonely person in the room who needs a friend and a little cheering up!

Be considerate of others by putting yourself in their shoes!

*Especially out in public, people tend to be a little nervous. Part of having good manners is trying to put people at ease by being ourselves and really getting to **know** them. Think of what Jesus would do in your situation!*

Always look for something positive to say.

*Be grateful! Smile, laugh, and above all...treat others as **you** would like to be treated. ☺*

TIME TO THINK!

1. What should a girl do if she finds she has used the wrong tableware?

_____

_____

_____

2. What are some of the obligations of a hostess?

_____

_____

_____

3. What are a few conversation "No No's"?

_____

_____

_____

4. What are some mannerly things a girl can do while she is at a party?

_____

_____

_____

5. How should people act while they are in public?

_____

_____

_____

6. Why is it important to practice good manners?

_____

_____

_____

What About Me?

1. Do I make a conscience effort to be aware of the feelings of others around me when I'm in public? Why or why not?

_____

_____

2. Do I visit with as many people as possible at a party? If not, why?

_____

_____

_____

3. Do I demonstrate an "attitude of gratitude" on a regular basis?

_____

_____

4. In what ways can I become more grateful?

_____

_____

_____

5. When I have guests over, do I follow the guidelines of a proper Hostess?

_____

_____

6. What is the first thing I should do when I sit down at a table to eat?

_____

_____

7. How can I have meaningful conversations with others?

_____

_____

_____

Role Models

It can be hard to find good role models in this world! People strive to be rich and famous like the movie stars or athletes. We should look to Jesus Christ, first and foremost! *He* is the best example there is. His character should be the highest standard of living.

We need to be very careful who we aspire to be like in this world. Role models need to earn our respect through their words, behavior, and deeds. God gave us an entire Book full of people who lived lives that we can learn lessons from. Some of them have taught us how not to live, and others lived lives that the Lord blessed. Why don't you look at some of the Godly women from the Bible? These women had strong character. Why not make role models of them?

1.   Ruth *(Ruth 1-4)*

2.   Esther *(Esther 1-10)*

3.   Abigail *(I Samuel 25:2-44)*

4.   Lydia *(Acts 16:11-15)*

6.   Mary, Lazarus' sister *(Luke 10:38-42 & John 11, 12:1-8)*

YOUR ASSIGNMENT

Pick a woman from the Bible (it doesn't have to be one of the women listed above) and read her story. Write a small paper on her life answering these questions about her:

- *What makes this woman different from other women I see today?*

- *What Godly or ungodly characteristics did she demonstrate in her life?*

- *In what areas can I be like her in my own life?*

- *Were there any struggles in her life that she had to overcome to continue to serve the Lord? What were they, and how did she respond to them?*

Like Women of the Bible...

Like **Deborah**, I will serve the Lord in power and speak His word without fear.

Like **Esther**, I will intercede for God's people before the throne.

Like **Abigail**, I will humble myself to wash the feet of the servants of the Lord.

Like **Sarah**, I will respect my spouse and his ministry to the Lord.

Like **Hannah**, I will dedicate my children to the Lord.

Like **Priscilla**, I will explain the way of God more perfectly to those who are seeking.

Like the **Shunamite widow**, I will trust God in the day of adversity.

Like **Lydia**, I will be a worshiper of God and open my home to His ministers.

Like **Tabitha (Dorcas)**, I will always do good and help the poor.

Like **Joanna**, I will use my wealth to support the ministry of Jesus.

Like **Mary**, the mother of Jesus, I will hear the word of God to me and will answer,
"Be it unto me as you have said."

Like **Mary, the sister of Martha**, I will know the voice of Jesus and hear His words.

Like **Mary, the mother of Mark**, I will make my home a haven for the followers of Jesus.

Like **Mary, the Magdalene**, I will keep at the feet of Jesus and love Him unto death.

~ *Author Unknown*

~ LOVE ~

From the Dictionary . . .

To hold dear; to cherish; take pleasure in; the fatherly concern of God for man.

How You Can Live It . . .

Learn how to give to other's needs by putting your own wants aside.

How Jesus Christ Lived a Life of Love . . .

"I [Jesus] command you to love each other in the same way that I love you. And here is how to measure it - the greatest love is shown when people lay down their lives for their friends." ~ John 15:12-13 (NLT)

Christ demonstrated His **LOVE** for us with the ultimate sacrifice of dying on the cross for our sins. Shouldn't we be willing to give of ourselves for others? ☺

~ FORGIVENESS ~

From the Dictionary . . .

The act of forgiving. (Forgive: to cease to feel resentment against an offender.)

How You Can Live It . . .

Remember that God allows benefit in your life through the pain others cause you! ☺

How Jesus Christ Lived a Life of Forgiveness . . .

"Finally, they came to a place called The Skull. All three were crucified there — Jesus on the center cross, and the two criminals on either side. Jesus said, 'Father, forgive these people, because they don't know what they are doing...'" ~ Luke 23:33-34 (NLT)

Psalm 103:12 says that God throws the sins we confess to Him as far as the east is from the west! He is faithful to forgive us, no matter how many times we fail Him. (1 John 1:9) Jesus was the perfect example of forgiveness as He hung on the cross in agony, interceding for His offenders to the very end.

~ OBEDIENCE ~

From the Dictionary . . .

Submission to the restraint or command of authority.

How You Can Live It . . .

Follow the wishes of God, your parents, and others in authority.

How Jesus Christ Lived a Life of Obedience . . .

" 'Father, if You are willing, please take this cup of suffering away from Me. Yet I want Your will, not Mine.' "
~ Luke 22:42 (NLT)

> Jesus was willing to submit and to obey His Father no matter the cost. He suffered of His own accord. He knew that obedience meant the path to the cross. We should follow Jesus' example in our own lives when it comes to obeying our Heavenly Father, as well as our authorities on this earth.

~ HUMILITY ~

> *"It is a wonderful day indeed when we stop working for God and begin working with God."*
> *~ Max Lucado*

From the Dictionary . . .

Not proud or haughty; not arrogant or assertive.

How You Can Live It . . .

Quickly give praise back to God and other people. Understand that you are powerless apart from Christ! ☺

How Jesus Christ Lived a Life of Humility . . .

"Don't you believe that I am in the Father and the Father is in Me? The words I say are not My own, but My Father who lives in Me does His work through Me." ~ John 14:10 (NLT)

> Jesus realized that He was an instrument in the Hands of His Father. Every good and perfect gift comes from above. We are *nothing* without *His* strength! ☺

~ COMPASSION ~

From the Dictionary . . .

Sympathetic consciousness of other's distresses, together with a desire to alleviate it.

How You Can Live It . . .

Learn to feel the hurts of others, and do your best to relieve the pain they are experiencing.

How Jesus Christ Lived a Life of Compassion . . .

"Suddenly, a man with leprosy approached Jesus. He knelt before Him, worshiping. 'Lord,' the man said, 'if You want to, You can make me well again.' Jesus touched him. 'I want to,' He said. 'Be healed!' And instantly the leprosy disappeared." ~ *Matthew 8:2-3 (NLT)*

Can you imagine what kind of life the leper must have lived being declared "unclean" for much of his life? And then the Son of God came around the corner! Jesus showed the ultimate act of *compassion* by reaching out His healing hand and touching this poor, needy leper. We too, need to reach out the hand of compassion to those who are desperate for love! (Colossians 3:12)

~ JOYFULNESS ~

From the Dictionary . . .

Experiencing, causing, or showing joy; being happy and glad.

How You Can Live It . . .

Learn how to cheer the hearts of others! ☺ Do your best to be content in any circumstance.

How Jesus Christ Lived a Life of Joyfulness . . .

"Many Samaritans from the village believed in Jesus because the [Samaritan] woman had said, 'He told me everything I ever did!' When they came out to see Him, they begged Him to stay at their village. So He stayed for two days, long enough for many of them to hear His message and believe." ~ *John 4:39-41 (NLT)*

The Samaritan woman could no longer endure her life the way it was. She came to the well in the heat of the day when no one else would be there to ridicule her. Jesus offered her *living water*. He brought *joy* into her life and she shared that joy with everyone she came in contact with. Joy is contagious! Infect as many as you can!! ☺ (John 4:1-42 & James 1:2)

TIME TO THINK!

LOVE

1. When you are with other people, are you envious of what they have?

_____

_____

FORGIVENESS

2. Have you looked for ways to invest in the life of someone who has hurt you?

_____

_____

OBEDIENCE

3. Does your family see you obeying God on a day-to-day basis? Why or why not?

_____

_____

HUMILITY

4. Are you able to give the glory to God when you are praised for your accomplishments?

_____

_____

COMPASSION

5. Do you make jokes at the expense of others?

_____

_____

JOYFULNESS

6. Are you able to greet everyone with a smile, even when you don't feel like smiling? If not, why?

_____

_____

_____

What About Me?

LOVE

1. How can I go out of my way to love those who are hard to love?

_____

_____

FORGIVENESS

2. Do I hold unforgiveness in my heart towards others who have hurt me? Who has hurt me?

_____

_____

_____

OBEDIENCE

3. In order to obey God, are there some things I should be doing? (Name both little and big things.)

_____

_____

_____

HUMILITY

4. Am I able to accept criticism without resentment?

_____

_____

COMPASSION

5. How do I respond to people who have physical and mental handicaps?

_____

_____

JOYFULNESS

6. How cheerfully do I greet my family members in the morning?

_____

_____

Chapter 5

‹›‹› ‹›‹›

She should <u>know</u> that she has been given talents and abilities by God as a way to bless those He will bring across her path.

‹›‹› ‹›‹›

"The eyes of your understanding being enlightened; that ye may <u>know</u> what is the hope of His calling…" ~ Ephesians 1:18 (KJV)

ℰℭ

God's Gifts

Whether you know it or not, you have God-given talents and abilities! ☺ Yet, there are things that we all would like to change about ourselves. Always remember...God *never* makes mistakes. He made you just the way He wanted and He *loves* you!!

"...I am fearfully and wonderfully made..." ~ *Psalm 139:14 (NIV)*

There are many things about ourselves that we cannot change! Some examples would be our family members, whether or not we are born a boy or a girl, our mental abilities, the fact that we will all die eventually, etc.

It is important to be content with the fact that we can't change these things! They are given to us so that we can learn to trust Him...no matter what He sends our way! He wants you to give Him your all. Not just a little bit, but *everything*.

If you have accepted Jesus Christ as your Savior, then you have been given one or more spiritual gifts. Spiritual gifts (also known as "grace gifts") are given to Christians to demonstrate *His* love to those around us. (See 1 Corinthians 12 and Ephesians 4:8, 12-13) There are different types of spiritual gifts, but we will be discussing the ones listed in Romans 12:4-8:

"Just as each of us has one body with many members, and these members do not all have the same functions, so in Christ we who are many form one body, and each member belongs to all the others. We have different gifts, according to the grace given us. If a man's gift is **prophesying***, let him use it in proportion to his faith. If it is* **serving***, let him serve; if it is* **teaching***, let him teach; if it is* **encouraging [exhorting]***, let him encourage; if it is* **contributing to the needs of others [giving]***, let him give generously; if it is* **leadership [organizing]***, let him govern diligently; if it is showing* **mercy***, let him do it cheerfully." (NIV)*

Many of the conflicts we experience with others (specifically those in our family) are most often the result of a misunderstanding of another's Spiritual gift, or a misuse of that gift. Who knows? Maybe you are misusing *your* gift?

We should all be sensitive to the needs of others, and try to put ourselves in their shoes. Ask yourself why they do the things they do. So...do you know what your spiritual gift is? Let's take a look at the characteristics of these gifts and some situations you may experience to see what your spiritual gift(s) may be! ☺

A Spiritual Gift Breakdown...

Prophecy	A Prophet's driving force: *Sharing the truth no matter the cost.*	
"But speaking the truth in love..." ~ Ephesians 4:15 (KJV)	- *Decisive and firm* - *Leads others well* - *Extremely passionate* - *Occasional negativity* - *Quick conclusions* - *Good judge of character* - *Can lack sensitivity* - *Deep sense of justice / right and wrong*	My Mom and brother Marc are both Prophets. My brother Logan has some tendencies for this spiritual gift too. So needless to say, it can be really *fun* when they all get together! ☺ Nothing else seems to matter much except the *truth* of a situation. It's awesome because they can really cut right to the "meat" of an issue. I like seeing that in my Mom and brothers. ☺

Serving	A Servant's driving force: *Working to fulfill any type of need.*	
"...but by love serve one another." ~ Galatians 5:13 (KJV)	- *Quickly sees what must be done* - *Wants to take care of needs* - *Ignores own physical weariness* - *Must feel appreciated* - *Sometimes gives unwanted help* - *Remembers what others like* - *Can resent ungratefulness* - *Invests self into chores*	My Grandma Cox is one of the best examples of a Servant that I can think of. Rarely do I see her taking time for herself, but she's constantly doing special things for other people. ☺ For years I've admired her ability to remember what so many people like and dislike! She also enjoys doing nice little things for people "just because".

Teaching	A Teacher's driving force: *Learning and sharing new facts.*	
"Study to show thyself approved unto God..." ~2 Timothy 2:15 (KJV)	- *Likes details (very perfectionist)* - *Thorough!* - *Presents facts in a systematic way* - *Easily works out misunderstandings* - *Tempted to argue over minor details* - *Pride caused by knowing so much*	I appreciate a Teacher's attention to details. They have a way of just throwing themselves *wholeheartedly* into something they're interested in (sometimes like their very life depends on it)! ☺ That's a wonderful quality and is one that I'm trying to follow because it's often frightfully scary how very "non-detail oriented" I can be! ☺

Exhorter

*"But **exhort** one another daily while it is called Today…"*

~ Hebrews 3:13 (KJV)

An Exhorter's driving force: *Encouraging others to look to the future.*

- Needs visuals to understand
- Paints clear mental pictures for others
- Can set unrealistic goals
- Needs to share face-to-face
- Committed to growing in the Lord
- Looks toward the future
- Can be insensitive to people's feelings

Want to see a true-blue Exhorter?? Well, meet my Dad! ☺ The little things right here and now usually don't get him down, because he rests in knowing God's going to work all things out for good.

It's nice to have the levelheaded response of an Exhorter when it comes to some of the silly situations I often get all bent out of shape over! ☺ Yep, Exhorters are *great* encouragers.

Giving

*"**Do not withhold good** from those who deserve it, when it is in your power to act."*

~ Proverbs 3:27 (NIV)

A Giver's driving force: *Seeing and meeting visible needs.*

- Fulfills material needs
- Has wisdom in financial giving
- Invests self into every contribution
- Enjoys giving all kinds of gifts
- Sometimes give to projects vs. people
- Wants quality in presents
- Frugality can turn into stinginess

We should all try to be like Givers, because they invest of themselves in every gift they give. ☺ Also, I'm amazed at how sensitive Giver's are to the voice of God! They listen to the Lord when He lays a need on their hearts, time after time giving the perfect gift at the *perfect* time.

Givers often like to remain anonymous so only God knows about their act of love. Now, I think that's neat! ☺

Organizing

*"Let all things be done decently and in **order**."*

~ 1 Corinthians 14:40 (KJV)

An Organizer's driving force: *Getting the most done in the most efficient way.*

- Has the finished project in mind
- Leads by example
- Efficiency is a must
- Sometimes makes a job look too easy
- Volunteers to head up projects
- Can put projects ahead of people
- Knows the best person for each job

Organizers know how to get the job done! ☺ My Aunt is an Organizer, and she's always telling me about some new project she's working on at her church or in the community. It makes me smile. ☺ She truly enjoys leading and planning big things!

And once again, I'm not at all like that (although I wish I was!). Thank God for making us all different!

Mercy

*"…live in harmony with one another; be **sympathetic**… be **compassionate**, and humble."*

~ 1 Peter 3:8 (NIV)

A Mercy's driving force: *Taking away pain.*

- Wants to relieve hurts and pains
- Needs true friendship
- Can fail to be firm or decisive
- Attracts people who are hurting
- Sometimes referred to as "gullible"
- Often relies on feelings vs. reason
- Doesn't want to hurt anyone

Okay, I can't hide it any longer. This one's me. ☺ Yes, I'm a Mercy! That means I feel things very deeply. I'm also indecisive and extremely gullible (sometimes jokes go right over my little head ☺). But you can be sure of one thing: if you need a shoulder to cry on, call on a Mercy. We'll come and let you cry all you want!! ☺

I once heard a story that illustrated how people might respond in light of their spiritual gifts. I thought it was a fun way to help us understand more about how these gifts are seen and demonstrated in everyday life. Maybe it will do the same for you! So, read and enjoy. *(Oh, and this is Myklin's free-translation...☺)*

Let's say you are at your brother's birthday party having the time of your life, right? Before you know it, it's time for your sister to bring out the cake. This is no ordinary cake, either! This cake is top of the line, double layered, triple thick, Chocolate Fudge Brownie Extreme! We're talkin' MMMmmmm, good. ☺

So you're partying away...just minding your own business, when all of a sudden, your sister (who has slaved hours and hours on this masterpiece of a cake) comes through the kitchen door. But me oh my, she *trips* on the very edge of the rug, thus losing her grip on the cake platter, causing the beautifully perched masterpiece to slide from it's position of greatness, smack dab onto the living room floor.

Ruined. Completely ruined. As everyone stares in shock and disbelief, all you can think about is how *good* that cake would have tasted right about now! Oh, the disappointment! But now you have several choices. You can respond in many different ways. What would you say if this happened to you? What would your first response be? Remember, this is your *sister* you're talking to!! ☺

1. "Mom said not to carry that by yourself! See what happens when you don't listen?"

2. "Here, I'll take care of that. You guys go on with the party."

3. "The reason that happened was because she wasn't carrying it level."

4. "Everything will be okay. Next time we'll just eat the cake in the kitchen."

5. "I'm on my way to go buy a new dessert. I'll be back in a few minutes."

6. "Kate, would you grab a dish rag? Joe, please go get the stain remover. I'll get the dog."

7. "I'm sorry! You worked so hard on that cake! Do you need a hug?"

8. "_____"

86

WHAT WOULD *YOUR* RESPONSE BE?

- If you chose number 1, you would be thinking like a Prophet. You would have felt it your duty to state the facts as clearly as you see them, thus doing your best to correct the problem. *(Remember, the Prophet tells the truth — no matter what!* ☺*)*

- If you chose number 2, you would be showing a Servant's mindset. You would have tried to fulfill the need all by yourself if necessary *(forgetting your own needs* ☺*)*.

- If you were more likely to choose number 3, you would be siding with the Teacher. Your driving force would be to understand why this happened in the first place. *(Teachers like the facts.* ☺*)*

- If you think number 4 sounds more like you, you would be showing the Exhorter's spiritual gift. The Exhorter would be thinking of fixing future problems. *(Remember...they are focused on how everything will end!* ☺*)*

- If you feel that number 5 would be your response, you would be driven by the gift of Giving, thus trying to meet a material need of the group. *(The Giver is willing to use his or her own money if need be, to get the job done!* ☺*)*

- If you chose number 6, you would be demonstrating the Organizer's spiritual gift. You would want to achieve the goal as efficiently and quickly as possible! *(Although you probably shouldn't call on the dog for cleanup seeing as it's a chocolate cake and dogs shouldn't eat chocolate.* ☺*)*

- If you feel like number 7 sounds more like you, then you would be leaning to the Merciful side of spiritual gifts. Your motivation would be to lessen any embarrassment or sadness caused by the accident. *(This is where I would be giving hugs and making jokes to lighten the mood, so that nobody would be getting upset!)*

Consider your first response and see what your motivation behind it would be. There are many situations that you could use to test your reaction. The thing to remember is that we should strive to be like Jesus Christ who demonstrated all these gifts beautifully. ☺

One way to discover your spiritual gift is to just get out there and *work!* Whatever you put your hand to, work at it with your whole heart! It may not be until a later date that you can step back to see what area you were able to do your best and be the most effective. It took me a long time to discover that my spiritual gift is Mercy. And even now I am not completely 100% Mercy, but a mixture of a couple others, which is a good thing! We should just do our best to be like Jesus, no matter what. ☺

"As every man [or woman] hath received the gift, even so minister the same one to another, as good stewards of the manifold grace of God. If any man speak, let him speak as the oracles of God; if any man minister, let him do it as of the ability which God giveth: that God in all things may be glorified through Jesus Christ, to whom be praise and dominion forever and ever. Amen."

~ 1 Peter 4:10-11 (KJV)

What Talents & Abilities Has God Given You?

Every person is unique! ☺ Some people are able to do long math calculations in their heads, others can sing like angels, and still others are great with people. What can *you* do unlike anyone else? What are some gifts that you have been given that you can share with others?

> *"Every good gift and every perfect gift is from above, and cometh down from the Father of lights, with whom is no variableness, neither shadow of turning."* ~ James 1:17 (KJV)

Below are a few basic areas that may help you understand a little more about what interests you. Keep in mind that these are just generalizations. For example, if you're like me, you might have an interest in sports, but may not be particularly gifted in that area! ☺ There is a difference between enjoying something and having a natural talent for it. We can learn to like anything and eventually be good at it, if we are persistent and committed. Don't feel discouraged if some skill doesn't come as easily for you as it does for the next person!

You are special just the way you are!! ☺

<table>
<tr>
<td rowspan="2">

THE ATHLETE

</td>
<td>

- *Good at sports*
- *Health & nutrition nut* ☺
- *Early to rise*
- *Unwilling to give up or quit*
- *Enjoys exercising & working out*
- *Lives a scheduled / disciplined life*
- *Early to bed*

</td>
<td>

</td>
</tr>
</table>

Does This Sound Like You?

True athletes live very disciplined lives full of strength and commitment to their sport or routine. These qualities are very admirable and should be emulated in all areas of our lives. What are a few ways that someone with these talents could use their abilities to bless others & serve God?

_____

_____

THE SCHOLAR

- *Intrigued by the details of projects*
- *Academic studies come fairly easy*
- *Better at writing out thoughts than verbalizing them*
- *Mathematically inclined*
- *Naturally good at teaching others*

Does This Sound Like You?

The academically minded person lives to discover new and exciting things about his or her area of expertise. They can often remember important details and are extremely "perfectionistic". How could someone use their great academic abilities to glorify God and benefit others?

_____

_____

THE ARTIST

- *Has musical talents (singing, playing an instrument, writing music, etc.)*
- *Listens to the details of music*
- *Has artistic abilities*
- *Drama / Theatrical interests*
- *Can listen intently to sounds and hear things most people miss*

Does This Sound Like You?

Have you ever heard the term "Temperamental Artist"? You probably have because it is often very true of artists! ☺ They feel extremely passionate about what they do, usually becoming entirely engrossed in it. How could a musician, actor, or artist use their talents for the Lord? Are there any spiritual dangers they might have to overcome? If so, what are they?

_____

_____

THE SOCIAL BUTTERFLY

- *Has good leadership skills*
- *Good at public speaking*
- *Gives clear instructions*
- *Natural leadership abilities*
- *Can do well in debates*
- *Makes friends easily*
- *An outgoing personality*

Does This Sound Like You?

A social butterfly (also known as a "people person") is usually a good communicator. Often they are able to rally people behind them to accomplish a task. They have a spark to their lives that attracts others. How could this person use their skills to direct people's attention back to the Lord?

_____

_____

THE WORKER

- *Content to be a follower*
- *Sees things that need to be done*
- *Glad to go without recognition*
- *Befriends "misfits" or lonely people*
- *Not a loud or showy personality*
- *Likes to be a "completer" to the leader*

Does This Sound Like You?

This individual can also be called a "behind the scenes" person. These people have no desire to be in the so-called limelight. They enjoy being a quiet person that no one sees or sometimes even knows about! They may be tempted to give into shyness, but the best Worker is one who has learned the balance of listening and speaking. They can also seek out those who are lonely and need a friend. How could a Worker turn people's attention back to the Lord?

_____

_____

Were you able to see yourself in any of those categories? If not, then don't worry. ☺ This isn't an all-inclusive list of every skill and talent in the world, by any means! Hopefully you now have a few ideas. What you should do is just get out there and do your absolute best at whatever is put in front of you!

I know many people downplay whatever talents or abilities God has given them, because they feel unworthy of something that seems so impressive. I heard a quote once that really stuck with me that went something like this:

"God doesn't call the equipped; He equips the called."

That should make us think. Just look at the life of Moses! God called him to deliver a message of freedom and deliverance from bondage to the Israelites. Moses told the Lord he couldn't do it because he didn't speak very well. (Boy, I understand that! ☺) But did that keep God from using ol' Moses?? Not at all! God used Moses in a *powerful* way. (Exodus 3:10-14)

He wants to do the same with you! So girls, I pray that you will allow yourself to be used of the Lord. He *will* bless you for it.

"Whatever you do, work at it with all your heart, as working for the LORD,
not for men." ~ Colossians 3:23 (NIV)

10 Ways to Become a Blessing to Those Around You...

1. Look for ways to serve. *(Matthew 20:27)*

2. Be positive and enthusiastic in words and in actions. (Proverbs 17:22)

3. Exhibit gratefulness for the small things. Try writing thank you letters! *(1 Corinthians 1:4)*

4. Be the first to accept responsibility or say you are sorry. *(II Timothy 2:24-25)*

5. Be generous with praise by commending character! *(Proverbs 25:11)*

6. Be there to listen in the good times and the bad. *(Proverbs 17:17)*

7. Be open about your own faults. *(Colossians 3:12-13)*

8. Ask others if there are specific requests that you can pray for them. *(I Thessalonians 1:2-3)*

9. Do things to let people know that they are special to you. Prepare favorite meals, give gifts out of season, do something fun or out of the ordinary, etc.! *(Ephesians 4:32)*

10. Ask the Lord to give you a *true love* for those around you. *(I John 3:23)*

"Finally, all of you, live in harmony with one another; be sympathetic, love as brothers, be compassionate and humble. Do not repay evil with evil or insult with insult, but with blessing, because to this you were called so that you may inherit a blessing." ~ 1 Peter 3:8-9 (NIV)

Think about the condition of your heart. Do you strive to put your wants and desires first or do you care about people God has placed around you? How about your family members? What do they see of your heart on a day-to-day basis? Do you often treat the ones you love unkindly? What can you do to become a blessing wherever God has placed you? ☺ Think of some people you know who are in need of encouragement. Why not write a "thank you" letter to those who have meant a lot to you over the years or who have made sacrifices on your behalf? ☺ If you don't know what to say, ask the Lord to show you and believe me...He will!!

TIME TO THINK!

1. What is the driving force of an Exhorter?

   a. Working to fulfill any type of need
   b. Encouraging others to share the truth no matter the cost
   c. Taking away pain
   d. Encouraging others to look toward the future

2. A person with this spiritual gift enjoys remaining anonymous:

   a. Organizing
   b. Teaching
   c. Giving
   d. Prophecy

3. Which person enjoys the details of a project?

   a. The Scholar
   b. The Worker
   c. The Social Butterfly

4. What is a characteristic of The Athlete?

   a. Outgoing personality
   b. Early to rise and early to bed
   c. Content to be a follower

5. What does Hebrews 11:24-29 say about how God used Moses to do His work?

_____

_____

6. Name 3 ways you can become a blessing to those around you:

_____

_____

_____

What About Me?

1. What is my spiritual gift(s)?

_____

2. How can I use this gift(s) to glorify God?

_____

_____

_____

_____

3. What talents and abilities do I possess?

_____

_____

_____

_____

4. Are there skills that I'm weaker in than others? What are they?

_____

_____

_____

5. What are some more ways I can encourage and bless others?

_____

_____

_____

6. Who are some people I know that need to be encouraged by me?

_____

_____

Home Economics

Okay! So we know that God has given us all talents and abilities. Some things we are naturally better at than others. But does that mean we should only know how to do what comes naturally to us?? I don't think so! ☺ God wants us to be versatile. Be all things to all people! (1 Corinthians 9:22) True, we must know our limitations, but still always strive to be all that we can be!

I know people who don't think they're very good at cooking, baking or household things, so they don't even try! This next section we will discuss the bare essentials of Home Economics. We could very easily spend an entire course on this one subject alone, so needless to say…this will be the condensed version!!

My Mother very graciously agreed to help me out with this section. For although I try my best, I still am not as adept in the kitchen and with household tasks as she is! After all, she is a mother. ☺ So I would like to say a big "thank you" to her, not only for writing this section with me, but for being such a wonderful example to me in the area of Home Ec. I love you, Mom. THANKS!

> *"She watches over the affairs of her household*
> *and does not eat the bread of idleness."*
> *~ Proverbs 31:27 (NIV)*

Cooking Terms and Definitions

Baste	To moisten food for added flavor and to prevent drying out while cooking.
Beat	To stir rapidly to make a mixture smooth, using a whisk, spoon or mixer.
Blend	To thoroughly combine two or more ingredients.
Bread	To coat with crumbs or cornmeal before cooking.
Broil	To cook on a rack or spit under or over direct heat, usually in an oven.
Chop	To cut food into small pieces, usually with a knife.
Cream	Beat ingredients, usually sugar and a fat, until smooth and fluffy.
Cube	To cut food into small, even pieces, usually about ½ inch.
Cut In	To distribute solid fat in flour using a cutting motion, with two knives or blender.
Deep Fry	To cook by completely immersing food in hot fat.
Drippings	Juices and fats rendered by meat or poultry during cooking.
Flute	To make decorative grooves; usually referring to pastry.
Fold	To combine light ingredients, like beaten egg whites, with a heavier mixture, using gentle over and under motion.
Glaze	To coat foods with glossy mixtures, such as jellies or sauces.
Grate	To rub food against a serrated surface to produce shredded or fine bits.
Knead	To blend dough together with hands or in a mixer to form a pliable mass.
Marinate	To soak in a flavored liquid; usually refers to meat, poultry or fish.
Mince	To cut into tiny pieces, usually with a knife.
Parboil	To boil until partially cooked.
Pare	To gently remove the outermost skin of a fruit or vegetable.
Poach	To cook gently in hot liquid kept just below the boiling point.
Puree	To mash foods by hand by rubbing through a sieve, or by whirling in a blender or food processor until perfectly smooth.
Refresh	To run cold water over food that has been parboiled, in order to stop the cooking process.
Sauté	To cook and/or brown food in a small quantity of hot shortening.
Scald	To heat liquid almost to a boil until bubbles begin to form around the edges.
Sear	To brown the surface of meat by quick cooking over high heat, in order to seal in the meat's juices.
Sift	To pass through a sieve, usually referring to flour, or powder substances.
Simmer	To cook in liquid just below the boiling point; bubbles form but do not burst on the liquid's surface.
Stew	To cook covered over low heat in a liquid.
Stir Fry	To quickly cook small pieces of food over high heat, stirring constantly.
Toss	To combine ingredients with a repeated lifting motion.
Whip	To beat food with a whisk or mixer to incorporate air and produce volume.

Safety in the Kitchen . . .

1. Always wash your hands before you start.

Scrub under your nails and between your fingers. The scrubbing motion is the best way to kill germs, then the soap washes them away. Wash your hands often during the cooking process. *(Don't use the same kitchen towel to dry both hands and dishes. Have separate towels or use paper towels to dry your hands.)* **It is especially important to scrub your hands and nails again after handling raw meat because it has a way of getting up under your nails!** Also, if you have a small cut or scratch on your hands, scrub it well too, even if it hurts! I know a lady who got food poisoning because bacteria entered a cut on her hand after she had been handling raw chicken. So...be careful girls!

2. Sanitize all areas of the kitchen.

One of your best defenses against bacteria in the kitchen is to have a spray bottle with a mixture of bleach and water at the sink at all times. Fill a small spray bottle (*not* the teeny tiny ones!) with water and add a ¼ teaspoon or less of bleach to it. If it smells *very* strong, then you have used too much bleach. Pour a little bit out of the spray bottle and add more water. Be careful not to get this on your clothes, tea towels or kitchen rags, as it could discolor them. However, if you use sponges or brushes in your kitchen, these should be sprayed with the bleach water after every cleanup. Sponges not only hide bacteria, but they can be a place where it will grow!

3. Never use the same cutting board for raw meat & fruits or vegetables.

Even if you wash the cutting board, there still may be remains of bacteria on it. After using raw meat on a cutting board, scrub it with soap and hot water (on both sides). Then spray both sides with bleach water and let it air dry in your drainer. It will then be ready for the next use. If you must use the same cutting board, only use it after you have completed this process. Wooden cutting boards are very likely to harbor bacteria. The newer cutting boards are made in such a way as to help stop bacteria growth on them. Next, spray down your kitchen counter with the bleach water mix. Let it set for a minute, then wipe it up with paper towels.

Common Sense . . .

- Keep cold foods cold and hot foods hot. Sounds simple, but it doesn't take much for the bacteria to grow, and grow rapidly! Take meat, eggs, milk, etc. out of the fridge just before you need them, unless the recipe calls for eggs or milk to be at room temperature. Bacteria will grow the most rapidly at room temperature.

- Sometimes when your meal is over, it is tempting to sit back, grab a cup of hot chocolate, and talk a while (especially when you have company). But don't delay too long! ☺ It's better to jump up and get the food put away quickly, and then you can take time to visit. Hot food needs to be rapidly cooled before storing in the fridge. Take soup or stew for example. If you have made a large pot and it still is very hot, you have a couple of options. First, you can divide the remaining soup into smaller containers, which will cool more rapidly in the refrigerator. Or, you can put your pot in the sink with cold ice water around it, making sure to stir it every so often. When it cools down enough, then you can put the whole pot in the fridge. Hot foods simply can't cool quickly enough when put in large containers and immediately placed in the refrigerator. Avoid doing this at all costs, girls! This is a sure fire way to get a yucky little thing called food born illness. ☹ When the pot is taken out and is ready to be re-heated, it is important to re-heat rapidly. Slowly bringing up the temperature of the food could (once again!) be a harbor for growing bacteria.

- If your kitchen does not have a meat thermometer, then you need to get one! They are inexpensive and can tell you how well your meat is cooked, even if it looks done. Most bacteria or E-Coli germs are killed at 170 degrees F. Make sure your cooked dishes reach this temperature. Leftovers must be re-heated to this temperature also.

- Never walk away from food cooking on top of the stove or in an electric skillet. If you must leave the room, turn off the heat from under the food. Kitchen fires can spread fast! At the very least, burned food leaves a horrible smell in the house and a very difficult pan to clean! If you have something in the oven and you must leave the kitchen, take your kitchen timer with you. "Out of sight, out of mind" is more than just a saying! Many good cooks have ruined a good batch of cookies because the phone rang, and they forgot them!

GOOD COOK-TOP HABITS

When cooking on the stovetop, watch all handles of pots and pans. Make sure they are turned inward, so that they can't be knocked off the stove. Burns from hot cooking food can be deadly. This is especially true if your family has young children. If your kitchen does not have a fire extinguisher, you need to get one of those, too! Fires can quickly get out of control, but the fast thinking cook can prevent disaster. Fire can also happen when you are taking baked items out of the oven. A dropped oven mitt can burst into flames very quickly. Knowing where the fire extinguisher is, and how to use it, can save lives and property!

Foods may actually cook better on low heat (and make less of a mess! ☺). You need high heat only to bring foods to a boil. Using a larger pan when cooking foods that foam - pasta, rice, milk, dried beans - will help you to keep them from boiling up and overflowing. *(Hint: a small pat of butter or margarine in the pot can keep pasta, rice, beans or potatoes from boiling over.)* When frying, use a small amount of oil and medium heat to keep the splatters to a minimum and to brown foods more evenly. Keep an eye on the food while it is cooking. If you must walk away, remove the pan and turn off the burner. Again, it's better to be safe than sorry! ☺

GOOD OVEN HABITS

To keep oven cleaning to a minimum, use a low temperature (325–350 degrees F) when cooking uncovered meats and poultry. There is less spattering, shrinkage is minimized, and the food will be juicy and flavorful. To prevent boiling over, don't fill pans too full. *(You can place a sheet of aluminum foil below the pan on a low rack to catch any drips.)* When using glass and glass-ceramic cookware, set the oven temperature 25 degrees lower than you would for metal cookware.

- All dry ingredients should be level unless you are directed to heap.

- Measure all flour according to the recipe, before or after sifting. Spoon a light amount into a measuring cup; be careful not to pack down the flour.

- Pour liquids in a clear glass or plastic measuring cup. Hold the cup at eye level to check the line for accuracy.

- Pack brown sugar firmly into a measuring cup.

- To use a meat thermometer properly, push the thermometer deep into the thickest part of your food. To get an accurate reading, wait until the dial on the thermometer has completely stopped rising.

- To chop or mince an onion, cut a slice from the end of a peeled onion and throw it away. Then divide the remaining end into little squares with a small knife. Slice the onion, and bingo!

- To melt chocolate pieces and squares, place chocolate in a small saucepan over very low heat. Stir very often, because there's nothing worse than scorched chocolate! ☺

- The best way to cut green beans is to hold a bunch of beans flat on a cutting board with your hand, and cut through them crosswise to make slices from ½ to 1 inch or longer.

- Always clean veggies or salad greens and keep them in the refrigerator. Fresh vegetables will only store for about a week, so be careful how long they sit in the bottom of your fridge! ☺ Remove all the discolored or brown leaves, but keep as many of the green leaves as possible. Dry them thoroughly before putting them in the refrigerator. Store in plastic zip-lock bags and then place in your refrigerator's crisper drawer.

MEASUREMENTS
1 tablespoon = 3 teaspoons
1/3 cup = 5 tbsp + 1tsp
1 cup dry = 16 tablespoons
1 quart = 4 cups
1 pound = 16 ounces
¼ cup = 4 tablespoons
1 cup liquid = 8 fluid oz
1 pint = 2 cups
1 gallon = 4 quarts

Baking A Cake...

1. Preheat

Before you mix anything (from scratch or from a mix), you must first preheat your oven. Most ovens have a preheat dial. Why preheat? The oven will reach the desired temperature quickly and evenly. Just be sure to change the preheat dial to bake before using the oven; otherwise the food is gooey on the bottom, and over done on the top!

2. Assemble all the ingredients

Set out everything you will need, from eggs and milk, to measuring cups and spatulas.

3. Mix according to directions

Read completely through the recipe and the directions first. Next, you'll want to mix your ingredients in the order the recipe says and in the way it says! This can actually make or break some cakes. Some recipes say the batter should be lumpy, therefore do *not* keep beating until all the lumps are gone. It changes the texture of the cake.

4. Bake

When baking 2 layer cakes, stagger the pans in the oven so that you have at least one inch between each pan as well as the sides of the oven. Even airflow is essential for the cake to bake properly. This is important for any item that you may be baking. Also make sure you have the proper size of pan for your recipe. Too large of a pan and the cake will be thin, dry and pale in color. Too small and well...you will have an ugly, smelly mess to clean up! Cakes baked in the right size pan will be golden brown in color and have a slightly rounded top.

How do you know when a cake is done? The most popular way is to take a toothpick and stick it in the middle of the cake. If it comes out "clean" (no batter sticking to it), it's ready to come out of the oven. Let the cake sit for about 10 minutes, then loosen the edges with a spatula.

5. Cool Completely

Take a knife and gently go around the edges of the cake while it is still in the pan. Place a cooling rack on top of the cake and turn the rack and the cake upside down. Lift off the pan, and place another rack lightly on top of the cake and turn both racks (with the cake between them) upside down. The top will now be right side up.

6. Frost

When it has completely cooled, gently frost it. Store cake in a container with a tightly fitting cover. If you do not have a cake keeper, turn a large bowl upside down over the cake. Enjoy!

Everyone loves cake! It is one of the easiest things for a cook to make. There are two kinds of cake types: cakes made from "scratch", and cakes from a package mix.

Cakes made from scratch have all the ingredients mixed by the cook. Cooks shouldn't think any less of themselves for making a packaged cake mix. Hungry people will *not* care how it was made! Do you want a cake to *taste* like it was made from scratch, when it really wasn't? Just make a special homemade frosting to put on it!

For instance, you could make a regular chocolate cake from a mix, bake it in a sheet cake pan, and make the special frosting that goes on a chocolate sheet cake. Everyone will love it and think you did it all from scratch. (After all, most good cooks have their own little secrets...just ask your mom! ☺)

Really, the only thing to remember about cooking or baking is: *if you can read, you can cook!* ☺ Check out what type of cookbooks you may already have around your house. Maybe your mom has a recipe file you could spend time browsing through, or start your own recipe file! You could decorate it to suit your own style. Make notes of recipes that you would like to try.

Another fun thing is to check out cookbooks from your local library. Most cookbooks have great information (i.e. helpful hints, time saving things to know, ways to substitute when you lack a certain ingredient, etc.)! ☺

From the Kitchen of: Myklin

Old-Time Yellow Cake

2¾ c sifted flour	1 tsp salt	3 eggs
1 tsp vanilla	2½ tsp baking powder	½ c butter
1½ c sugar	1 c milk	

Preheat oven to 350 degrees F. Grease and lightly flour 2 (9 X 1 ½-inch) round layer cake pans.

Combine flour, baking powder and salt in medium bowl. Beat softened butter and sugar in large bowl until soft and fluffy. Add eggs one at a time, beating well after each. Add vanilla. Stir in flour mixture little by little. Blend well. Pour half the batter into one layer pan, the other half into the second pan. Be sure to divide the batter equally between the two pans. Bake for 30-35 minutes. Test for doneness with toothpick.

From the Kitchen of: Myklin

Candy Caramel Sauce

| ½ pound caramel candy pieces (about 28) | ½ c hot water |

Place caramels and water in the top of a double boiler. Heat over boiling water, stirring frequently, until the caramels melt and make a smooth sauce. Serve hot or cold. Especially nice over ice cream or served with sliced apples. Yummy! ☺

From the Kitchen of: Myklin

Creamed Chicken

1 can condensed cream of chicken soup   2 c diced cooked chicken

1 / 3 c chicken broth   ¼ tsp salt

6 slices buttered toast

Mix the soup and broth in a saucepan. Add the chicken & salt. Heat the mixture until it is piping hot.

Spoon the hot chicken over the toast. Makes 6 servings.

From the Kitchen of: Myklin

Best-Ever Baked Potatoes

Scrub potatoes of the same size thoroughly with a brush. If you want them to have soft skins when baked, rub with cooking

oil. Wrap potatoes with foil and prick holes in them with a fork. Bake them on the rack in a hot oven at 450 degrees F, for

40-50 minutes, or until tender when stuck with a fork. When done, remove them from the oven at once. Cut a cross in the

top of the potatoes with a paring knife. Press the ends of each one to push out a little of the soft inner part. Break up inside

of potato with fork. Drop a square of butter or a spoonful of sour cream into the opening and serve immediately.

From the Kitchen of: Myklin

Tossed Garden Lettuce Salad

Wash and dry the leaves thoroughly. Tear the leaves into pieces the size of half dollars. Put the lettuce

in the bowl and sprinkle dressing on it - no more than 1 tablespoon of dressing to every serving of salad.

Toss the salad lightly with 2 forks or a fork and a spoon until you coat the leaves with the dressing. Add

bits of cooked bacon, diced fresh mushrooms, chopped carrot pieces, grated cheese, thin slices of

tomatoes, croutons, small chunks of cooked chicken, or sliced hard-boiled eggs.

From the Kitchen of: Myklin

Green Beans With Bacon

6 slices bacon	2 tablespoons tarragon or cider vinegar
½ tsp salt	6 tablespoons chopped onion
3 cups hot cooked green beans	

Cook the bacon until crisp, but not brittle. Lift it onto paper towels to drain. Pour out the bacon fat from the skillet.

Measure 3 tablespoons of fat back into the skillet. Add the onions and cook over low heat until soft, but not browned.

Add vinegar and salt. Place drained green beans in a serving dish and pour hot onion-vinegar mixture over them.

Crumble bacon over top. Serves 5 – 6.

From the Kitchen of: My friend, Brenda Nichols

Coconut Cream Cake

White Cake Mix	About 2 Cups Coconut
1 Small Tub of Cool Whip®	1 Can Sweet Condensed Milk

Bake cake according to mix directions. Let cool for approximately 10 minutes. Poke holes in cake with

the handle of a wooden spoon. Pour entire can of sweetened condensed milk over cake (make sure to fill

all the holes). Cool thoroughly. Spread whole tub of whipped cream evenly over cake. Top off by

sprinkling coconut over cake. In a 13x9 inch pan, it makes 12 large servings, or 15 moderate sized

servings. Keep refrigerated.

YOUR ASSIGNMENT!

Use the recipes on the previous pages or recipes of your own to prepare a meal for your family. The meal should include: vegetables, a side dish, a main dish, and a dessert. You don't have to make this very complicated. You most definitely don't have to prepare this meal completely by yourself! Just plan the menu and help to fix the meal. After you've finished, fill out the questions below.

1. **What did you prepare?**
• **Vegetable:**
• **Side Dish:**
• **Main Dish:**
• **Dessert:**
2. **What went smoothly?**
3. **What didn't go so smoothly?**
4. **What will you do differently the next time you prepare a meal?**
5. **What food item did everyone enjoy the most?**

Laundry Guidelines

1. First off, always start the cleaning process by reading the "tag" on the inside of the garment. Follow any special cleaning instructions listed there. ☺

2. Sort the clothes in a pile of "whites" and "colors," washing each pile separately to keep colors from all running together. (The whites and colors can also be further separated into delicate or fine washables and more sturdy washables.)

3. Always make sure you check the pockets of all the garments before throwing them in the washing machine! (You never know what kind of special treasures you may end up washing…thus ruining! ☹)

4. Turn the washing machine to the setting designed for the texture of the materials being washed.

5. Use the recommended amount of detergent. (Not too much, not too little!)

6. Rinse clothes very thoroughly after hand washing.

7. **Always remove the lint from the dryer's filter!** (This is very important because lint build up may be a fire hazard.)

How To Remove Stains

Ink: Use alcohol-free hair spray or Vaseline® followed by dry-cleaning solvent.

Antiperspirant: Rub liquid detergent into the stain, then wash in warm suds and rinse.

Blood: Wash stain immediately in cold running water, rubbing with plenty of soap, then rinse. If a stain is really hard to come out (or is old), soak it for 15 minutes in 2 tablespoons ammonia to every gallon of cool, soapy water. For remaining stains, soak in warm water mixed with an enzyme detergent. Wash in warm suds with a small amount of bleach, then rinse.

Butter/margarine: Stain usually comes out with ordinary laundering. If a greasy residue remains after washing, sponge or soak in dry cleaning solvent, then wash in warm suds. Rinse.

Ketchup/tomato sauce: Soak stain in cool water, followed by a wash in warm suds and then rinse. A dry-cleaning solvent may need to be used if it feels greasy after washing.

SEWING & MENDING...

- ## Always have the proper supplies on hand for the job.

You should assemble a sewing basket that includes all the emergency tools to mend, sew, pin or cut whatever is needed. The items below can be found at most department stores:

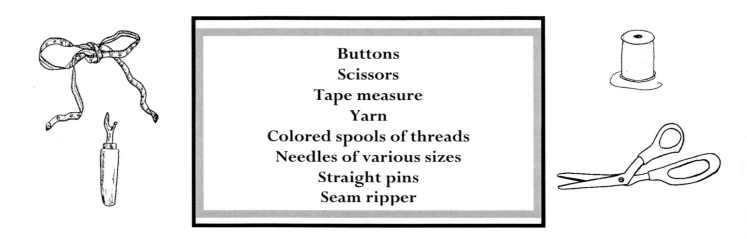

> **Buttons**
> **Scissors**
> **Tape measure**
> **Yarn**
> **Colored spools of threads**
> **Needles of various sizes**
> **Straight pins**
> **Seam ripper**

- ## Keep your supplies organized and inventoried.

Always know what mending and sewing supplies you have in stock. Use clear plastic organizing boxes to sort out everything you use. Make sure you keep the things that you use most often close by and easy to grab! ☺

- ## Remember, a stitch in time saves nine!

Don't put off mending the hole in your sock until the hole is twice the size of your house! ☺ When you first see the hole, mend it right away!! It will save you nine stitches (or more), in the long run.

Back Stitch

1. Knot your thread and pull the needle through the fabric at the point where you're going to begin sewing. You'll need to insert the needle an 1/8 of an inch behind the seam line point, and then pull it down through the fabric.

2. Next, bring your needle up through the fabric a 1/4 of an inch in front of your first stitch and insert it again right where the needle first came out.

3. Just keep up this stitching pattern, always making sure to insert the needle into the hole made by your previous stitch. (Without doing this, it won't have as much strength and it will no longer be called a "back stitch"! ☺)

This is a strong stitch and is recommended for hand-sewn seams. It can also be used for a nice finishing stitch.

Hem Stitch

This is simply a line of small, firm stitches.

1. On the wrong side of the garment, take a stitch in the hem edge.

2. Then take a stitch in the garment, picking up only one thread of the fabric, and bring the needle up through the hem edge coming out at least 1/4 inch ahead. Continue in this manner.

Running Stitch / Basting Stitch

1. Push the needle through both layers of fabric, going in and out several times before pulling the thread through.

2. Keep the stitches short and close together for a seam; long and widely spaced for basting.

A running stitch is a line of short, even stitches used for seams. A basting stitch is a long running stitch used for gathering or temporarily holding a hem or seam in place.

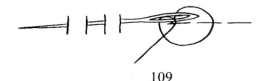

Sewing on Buttons

> There are two types of buttons: shank and sew-through. Sew-through buttons
> are the type with holes visible from the topside of the garment.
> Shank buttons are attached from underneath the button by a "shank",
> hence the name. Shank buttons give a garment a more finished look.

Sew-Through Buttons

1. First, you'll need to take a stitch or two directly where you will be sewing the button on your garment.

2. Then, from the underneath side of the garment, pull the thread up through one hole of the button, making sure to position the button in its proper place.

3. You'll need to continue to sew on the button going through each hole about five or six times to secure it tightly.

4. Next, take a few backstitches on the underneath side of the garment to secure the thread, then knot it tightly and cut off the extra thread.

Shank Buttons

1. Take a stitch or two at the place where you will be sewing on the button.

2. You'll then need to take five or six stitches through both the shank loop and the fabric. Take a few backstitches on the underneath side to make sure the thread is secured. Then knot it and cut the extra thread off.

TIME TO THINK!

1. Define:
   a. Sauté: _____
   b. Dice: _____
   c. Cream: _____
   d. Simmer: _____

2. What temperature should foods be cooked to?
   _____

3. How many ounces are in one pound?
   _____

4. How many teaspoons equal one tablespoon?
   _____

5. How many tablespoons equal 1/4 cup?
   _____

6. Brown sugar should be loosely measured into a cup.   True   False

7. Using more detergent ensures cleaner clothes.   True   False

8. Name one of the necessary basic stitches, and explain how/when it would be used:
   _____
   _____

9. Name the two different kinds of buttons:
   _____

10. Name one method used to remove ink from clothing:
    _____
    _____

11. When is the best time to treat stains?
    _____

What About Me?

1. When it comes to caring for a household what are my:

Strengths?	Weaknesses?

2. Am I able to accept correction in my areas of weakness? Why or why not?

_____

_____

_____

3. How can I help make things run more smoothly in my household?

_____

_____

_____

4. How am I going to do better this next week in the areas listed above?

_____

_____

_____

_____

> *"My idea of a super woman is someone who scrubs her own floor."* ~ Bette Middler

Chapter 6

ಐ ಐ

She should <u>know</u> that
her life is in the
Lord's Hands and
His timing is always perfect.

ಐ ಐ

"I <u>know</u> that Thou canst do everything, and that no thought
can be withholden from Thee." ~ Job 42:2 (KJV)

> *"I **know** that thou canst do everything, and that no thought can be withholden from Thee."*
> *~ Job 42:2 (KJV)*

Music From My Heart

I saw a cartoon once of a duck who was all tied up in ropes. He had this *scrunched* up facial expression that made me laugh when I saw it! Sometimes I feel like that duck, even though I hate to admit it! I can get pretty good at squirming, wiggling, and struggling to get out from under those silly ropes that seem to tie up my life and keep me from doing whatever I please. ☺ If I were to step back and look at myself during one of these particularly intense struggles, I would probably laugh hysterically at how silly I look!

God knew when He made us that we could choose to either live the way He would have us to live, or live within our own strength and power (which by the way, is not living at all; it's merely an existence!). Our "strength" will ultimately get us absolutely *nowhere*. God also knew that it often takes something very dramatic (or traumatic) to get our attention. It seems that only then are we willing to listen to His perfect plan.

Like me! I gave my life to Jesus Christ when I was quite young, but it wasn't until I was much older that I think I truly started trying to give "all" of me over to Him for *His* control.

You see, I *always* had this intense desire to play the piano, and not just for fun, but as a serious musician! God gave us a piano when I was seven, and by the age of ten I was learning how to play. Before long, I realized that this *had* to be my calling. *This* was my passion! I had great visions of performing in Carnegie Hall someday, with all my adoring fans enthralled by my music. I assumed that it *had* to be God's will for me, since it seemed so obvious.

Well...as is often the case, God had a different idea! ☺

I first noticed the pain the week I turned sixteen. It was hardly noticeable in the beginning, but it steadily increased. Shooting, stabbing, throbbing, *aching* pain all through my right hand! I couldn't understand it. Why all of a sudden? This mysterious pain would choose when to hurt and when not to. My doctors thought I was wacky, and sometimes I thought I was wacky, too!

Before long, I had to quit my beloved piano lessons. I remember leaving my last lesson and just crying my eyes out, wondering what in the world was happening to me!? This wasn't the way I had it planned. What about my wonderful plans? My future? My life?

By the next summer the pain had "spread" (if you could call it that) to my left hand as well. I had to quit everything: my job, teaching piano lessons, driving a car, writing, and even playing the piano for my own enjoyment. All of it was gone. I felt like part of me was gone. I couldn't understand what God was thinking. Everyone knew I was going to be a Concert Pianist, right?

I began to wonder if I had taken a few things for granted. Perhaps I had been a little hasty in planning my entire life. Oh yeah, and maybe I had forgotten the One who should be receiving all the glory from my accomplishments. And yes, maybe I had been a tad bit prideful in boasting in my own talent. Not just *maybe*, but *definitely!*

Oh, I saw it so clearly then! This was a test. A test that I had failed! From day one I had been playing for my own reward, all the time *thinking* I was really glorifying God. Granted, there were those times when I got up to perform that my heart really wanted God to be glorified, but my general attitude was that of pride. I had fooled myself and everyone else into thinking that my heart was pure before the Lord.

...I saw now it wasn't.

This was a test of my priorities. When something I loved dearly was taken away, would I cling to *it* rather than to *God?* Was I truly playing this music to have others look at the Lord, or at me? How often had the words "I," "me," or "mine" sprung to my lips? It had been about myself and so sadly, I had lost my focus on God.

I fell on my face and cried for forgiveness to the Lord! I didn't respond like Abraham who when asked to sacrifice his only son to the Lord, meekly answered in submission.

Here I was begging the Lord not to take away this one thing that was so dear to me away! And what happened to Abraham in the end? God spared his son because he *obeyed*, and was willing to sacrifice a beloved treasure (his son) for His Lord (see Genesis 22).

There is a song we occasionally sing in church that explains very well what it means to give God all the glory in worship. This concept can be applied to any area, not only to worship. The words to this song express what my heart is now singing to the Lord!

> *"I'm getting back to the heart of worship and it's all about You, Jesus;*
> *It's all about You. I'm sorry, Lord, for the thing I've made it.*
> *It's all about You, Jesus; It's all about **You**."*

Shouldn't that be our heart's song?! Everything should be about JESUS. Through my little testing, the Lord has shown me so many blessings that are too numerous to count! Yes, my hands are still in pain, and yes I'm unable to play the piano like I used to. But, you know what? It doesn't matter now! Jesus is my song! If I'm never able to play that song on the piano again, then I will just keep singing it in my heart until Jesus calls me to be with Him! I may never know exactly why God decided to remove something that I loved so dearly, but I am willing to never play again, as long as my Lord is here right beside me all the way.

So, the next time you begin to worry about your future, or you find yourself valuing something a little too highly, ask the Lord to help you make *Him* your only desire! Remember to never hold too tightly to anything or anyone in this life other than Jesus Christ. Go ahead and answer the questions on the next page and *please* be honest with yourself.

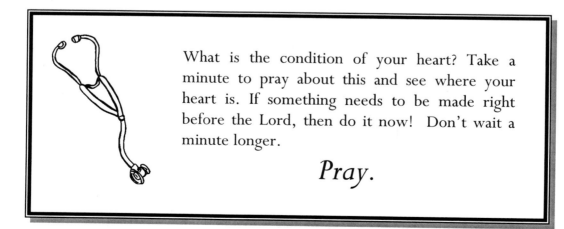

What is the condition of your heart? Take a minute to pray about this and see where your heart is. If something needs to be made right before the Lord, then do it now! Don't wait a minute longer.

Pray.

TIME TO THINK!

1. Read Genesis chapter 22:1-18.

2. What did God ask Abraham to do?

_____

_____

_____

3. What did Abraham do after God gave him a mission?

_____

_____

4. What kept Abraham from sacrificing his son (verses 10-13)?

_____

_____

5. According to verse 18, why did God bless Abraham?
   - a.) Because Abraham was a loving father
   - b.) Because Abraham had a joyful heart
   - c.) Because Abraham obeyed God even when he didn't understand

6. What would *you* have done in Abraham's situation?

_____

_____

_____

7. Has God ever taken away something you loved? If so, what was it and how did you respond?

_____

_____

_____

_____

What About Me?

1. Have I completely given my "all" to Jesus? If not, what is holding me back?

_____

_____

_____

_____

2. Do I struggle or fight inside when He asks me to do something I don't want to do?   What are those things He asks me to do?

_____

_____

_____

_____

3. What are some things in my life that I may have taken for granted?

_____

_____

4. Am I living as if I truly believe my future is in the Lord's Hands?

_____

_____

_____

5. Am I trying to be in control of the circumstances in my life? If so, in what way?

_____

_____

6. Is there something in my life that I value highly (maybe higher than Christ)? What is it?

_____

_____

_____

Where is Your Heart?

by Rene Walters

" 'You could have changed the world.'
These are the words spoken to one
Who like a spoiled child,
Desperately clutches a cheap thing desired
Only to find in the end,
He allowed the priceless to slip through his fingers.

The person who could have changed the world
Is satisfied with the good
And too afraid of what the best would cost him.
He is a servant
Who triumphantly recounts all that he has done,
Only to hear
'But you didn't do what I asked.'

God asks for a heart completely given to Him,
A heart that is not spurred on
By the onlookers' cries of praise,
But driven faster
By the whispers of strength
Found only in his Trainer's voice.

Does a rock know
The ripples it causes on a pond's surface?
Can we fully comprehend
The impact of a life completely dedicated to God?

The moment I live for
Is when my name will be called
To stand before the great throne of God,
And all of heaven is stilled
To hear the pronouncement.
Then, His voice like the ocean tide,
Will thunder through the holy city
And the angels' songs,
Like perfectly timed church bells, will ring.

He speaks,
'My child, you completed the race!'
But what of those
Who chose for themselves the words,
'The world would have been different,
If only you had given your heart to me.' "

> *"For the eyes of the Lord range throughout the earth to strengthen those whose hearts are fully committed to Him..."*
>
> ~ *2 Chronicles 16:9 (NIV)*

When Hard Times Come...

Inevitably, the day will come when you find yourself in over your head. Life can be full of many things; one of which is pain! As we talk about our future, we cannot skip over this very important fact about life, as much as we wish we could!

The Scriptures say if we love God, we *will* be tested. The mark of a mature Christian is testing. In John chapter 15, Jesus talks about a Pruner's shears coming along and cutting away mature branches that don't bear fruit. No doubt this cutting away is painful! Isaiah refers to testing as a "Refiner's fire"(Isaiah 48:10). As the fire heats the metal, all the impurities (or dross) come forth, only to be skimmed off the top. Then the metal is heated even more. Eventually the final product will be thoroughly refined, purified, and strengthened. But it wouldn't have become that way without the fire from the Refiner. The fire may be extremely painful, but the end result is *beautiful!*

One girl may seem to have small struggles when she compares her life to others. She may have fights with her parents, while another may be battling a disease, and yet another is being persecuted for her faith. What we need to remember is that God cares about *each one of us* - right where we are! Hurt is hurt. It hurts to fight with your parents, battle a disease, or be persecuted for your faith. What counts is that you are able to respond *positively* to God's testing in your life!

> *"No temptation has seized you except what is common to man [or woman].*
> *And God is faithful; He will not let you be tempted beyond what you can bear.*
> *But when you are tempted, He will also provide a way out so that you*
> *can stand up under it."* ~ *1 Corinthians 10:13 (NIV)*

We may be tempted to become bitter or angry because of the hurtful things that happen in our lives, but that's not the response Jesus wants us to have! Remember, we don't have to give in to those feelings of anger, despair, loneliness, or bitterness.

In whatever circumstance we find ourselves, we know that ultimately God desires to be glorified and honored through it. ☺ He may take each of us down different roads to get there, but in the end the result should be the same...to be more like His Son, Jesus. Yes, it hurts...sometimes more than it seems we can bear. But remember this: by *His* strength we can handle anything that comes our way. Let's keep in mind just a few of the reasons why pain comes into our lives.

WHY WE FACE HARD TIMES

1. *To bring about faith and perseverance in our lives.*

One reason we have trials in our lives is so that we may learn the character quality of endurance. The Bible says that life is one long race. Will we run in such a way as to win the race? Or somewhere along the way will we fall and not get up again? The course is rough, yet we must learn from the times we stumble and lose our footing! God desires that we trust His perfect plan, and believe by faith that He will see us through *whatever* comes our way! ☺ *(Philippians 3:12-14, Hebrews 12:1-3, and James 1: 2 — 6)*

2. *To bring into our hearts love and compassion for those who are hurting.*

God gives us circumstances to shape and mold us into the person we will someday become. Will we allow our pain to make us into someone consumed only with our self? Another reason we experience pain is so that we may learn to feel the hurts of others who are suffering. No matter how *bad* your life may be, if you stop and look around you'll see someone else who has it worse (although during your actual trial this may be hard to see)!

For example, my brother had to be in a wheel chair off and on for two years. Because of that, I will *never* be able to look at someone in a wheelchair the same way as before! I remember how much pain he was in at that time (both physically and emotionally), and it helps me to imagine what kind of pain they must be in. These things should develop in us a concern for those who are hurting, because we ourselves (or someone we love dearly) have experienced pain. *(1 Corinthians 13, Ephesians 5:2, Philippians 2:2-3, and 1 John 3:17-18)*

3. *To give God glory.*

God put us on this earth to give Him glory. Therefore it makes sense that everything in our life is designed to bring about the ultimate goal of *His* glory. Jesus suffered and died on the cross a brutally horrible death. Talk about a major *trial!* If He hadn't gone through all of the suffering and eventually death, how lost and utterly hopeless our lives would be!! God gives us trials of both big and little proportions. Why? So that we can respond in obedience to Him, and that *He* might receive all the glory! ☺ *(2 Corinthians 12:9 — 10, Ephesians 1:11 — 14, Philippians 1: 12 — 18, and 1 Peter 1:6 — 9)*

122

TIME TO THINK!

1. What are a few reasons suffering comes into our lives?

_____

_____

_____

2. How did Jesus Christ respond to suffering?
   - Persecution:

_____

   - Death of a friend:

_____

   - Physical pain leading to His own death:

_____

3. How should we respond to trials in our lives?

_____

_____

_____

4. Our Father in Heaven allows us to experience portions of suffering and pain, and He makes sure there's nothing we cannot handle through His strength.

   True   False

5. Scripture likens testings and trials unto:
   a) A Refiner's Fire
   b) A Pruner's Sheers
   c) A Race
   d) All of the above

What About Me?

1. What trials/sufferings have I gone through in the past?

_____
_____
_____
_____

2. What struggles am I currently going through?

_____
_____
_____

3. How do I respond to the situations the Lord has brought into my life?

_____
_____

4. In what ways am I going to respond better to the crisis's that come into my life?

_____
_____
_____

5. Can others see Jesus in my life through these hard times?

_____
_____

6. Am I resentful because of something that happened in my life? If so, why?

_____
_____
_____

7. How am I going to apply what I've learned here today this week?

_____
_____
_____

Please...make sure your heart is right with the Lord before finishing this chapter!!!

Has your heart been honoring to the Lord in the way it responds to difficult situations? If not, *why?* Let yourself be moldable in the Potter's faithful hands! He truly does know what is best for you. Can you trust Him with *all* of you? It's because of His *love* that He tests you. I pray you won't allow yourself to become bitter, hard, or angry because of the tough times He may send your way!

Please, let *Him* be your *joy!* The rewards are great when you can allow the difficulties in your life to draw you nearer to the Father's loving side. ☺

> *"I will be glad and rejoice in Thy mercy: for Thou hast considered my trouble;*
> *Thou hast known my soul in adversities;"* ~ Psalm 31:7 (KJV)
>
> *"It is good for me that I have been afflicted; that I may learn Thy statutes...*
> *I know, O Lord, that Thy judgments are right,*
> *and that Thou in faithfulness hast afflicted me."*
> *~ Psalm 119:71, 75 (KJV)*
>
> *"And not only so, but we glory in tribulations also: knowing that tribulation*
> *worketh patience; and patience, experience; and experience, hope:*
> *and hope maketh not ashamed; because the love of God is shed abroad*
> *in our hearts by the Holy Ghost which is given unto us.*
> *For when we were without strength, in due time Christ died for the ungodly."*
> *~ Romans 5:3-6 (KJV)*
>
> *"And we know that all things work together for good to them*
> *that love God, to them who are the called according to His purpose."*
> *~ Romans 8:28 (KJV)*
>
> *"For our light affliction, which is but for a moment, worketh for us a far more exceeding*
> *and eternal weight of glory;"* ~ 2 Corinthians 4:17 (KJV)
>
> *"That the trial of your faith, being much more precious than of gold that perisheth,*
> *though it be tried with fire, might be found unto praise and honor and glory at the*
> *appearing of Jesus Christ:"* ~ 1 Peter 1:7 (KJV)

Our Future and... Guys.

A discussion about God's planning for our lives just wouldn't be complete without mentioning young men and how *they* can impact our future! ☺ Some of you girls might be at a point in your life where a relationship with a guy is not too far away. Many of you may have years and years to wait before this is a reality for you! I just don't know. That's why we are simply going to discuss what the Bible says about being single young women.

If you are like me, then you have most likely been thinking about boys since you were quite young. I mean, how many girls *don't* sit around and dream about their wedding day and that special guy?? ☺ Believe me, it *is* an inevitable thought in every girl's mind. God designed us as women, and the majority of women have a romantic bone or two in their bodies. ☺ That's why my parents have been talking to me about guys for as long as I can remember!! They have been (and continue to be to this day) two of my truest sources of wisdom and encouragement in this area. They remind me of my responsibility as a single Christian young woman, and urge me to remain faithful to the Lord.

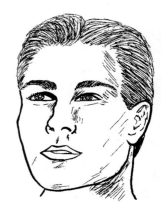

I know that some parents feel that it's best to wait to discuss courtship or dating with their daughters until they are in their teens, or ready to start a relationship of some kind. That is definitely a decision for each parent to make! God laid it on my parents' heart to begin to instill in me a desire to treat the guys around me with respect and purity at a young age. God calls different people to different things, and there is nothing wrong with that! ☺ So, in this section we will only discuss some basic points from Scripture about giving our single lives over to the Lord, and we'll just leave the details up to Mom and Dad!

As we look deeper into these issues, I would encourage you to truly consider the things I will share with you here. We may not see exactly eye to eye on these topics, but please take the time to listen and ponder these things carefully. ☺ Just because relationships have been done the same way for decades, doesn't necessarily mean that it's the right way. My way may not be the "right" way for someone else either! Who am I to say?

I only know what God wants *me* to do. I can't speak for you. I just pray that you will seek God's *best* for your life...whatever that may be! Don't let yourself settle for something that you feel in your heart is less than God's *best*.

So, I've already said that it's natural for us girls to think about boys quite a lot, but does that mean boys are *all* we need to think about? After all, it is only natural to have these feelings, right? Does this mean that we have to show how we feel about them every time one of them walks around the corner? <smiling> I would have to say no. Just because we feel a certain way doesn't mean we need to let those feelings and desires get in the way. What do I mean? Well, let's take a look! ☺

What is a girl's responsibility to the guys in her life?

> *"And let us consider how we may spur one another on toward love and good deeds."*
> *~ Hebrews 10:24 (NIV)*

What does this verse mean? Well, let's first look at a few definitions of words that may help us understand this concept better...

- **Defraud:** To cheat; To raise expectations that will not or cannot be fulfilled; Deception; To deprive of something through dishonesty.

- **Flirt:** To behave as if in love but without serious intent; To deal lightly with, or to play with; To trifle or toy with.

We all have seen them. (Who knows? Perhaps we have even *been* them!) Giggly, flirtatious girls who bat their eyes at all the boys, flip their hair teasingly, and who dress in the skimpiest items of clothing. They are everywhere you look! When I run into girls like this, I say a small prayer for them in my heart. I ask the Lord to show them the hurt that they may be setting themselves up for, as well as the hurt they may be setting those boys up for in the future.

Just think about it! If, while a certain girl is young, she flits from the arm of one boy to another (playing the ever popular "date and break" game), she is ultimately preparing herself for heartbreak in her future. ☹ When this girl eventually marries and begins to hit some of the inevitable bumps in the road of life, or she simply feels the need for someone or something new, what will keep her from turning right around and looking for her fulfillment with some other man? After all, that is how she did it all through her growing up years. It is sad that so many girls have completely put aside the fact that they should honor and respect young men as their brothers in Christ! Granted, if these young women don't know Jesus, then they will not understand what it means to treat the opposite sex as brothers in Christ. That's why we should set the example!

For many girls flirting and defrauding is as simple as breathing. To this kind of girl, liking a boy isn't often important. She gives a guy every indication that she likes him, but in reality she has no true intent in her heart. She may spend time laughing at this boy's jokes, teasing him, saying nice things to him, and doing other things that would indicate that she likes him. But truth be told, she's only having fun with him. This is *flirting*, which leads to *defrauding*, girls. We should stay as far away from this as possible! How are these things setting an example of purity and spurring one another on to love and good deeds? To put it simply: they're not. ☹

Have you ever considered that when you flirt, you may be defrauding the heart of another woman's *future husband??* That's a scary thought! But honestly, that's what's happening. ☹ Would you want another girl to be stirring up the heart of *your* future husband? I know I wouldn't! That's why we should help to guard the hearts of our brothers in Christ, as well as our own hearts, by avoiding flirtation and defrauding.

> *"Don't let anyone look down on you because you are young, but set an <u>example</u> for the believers in speech, in life, in love, in faith, and in purity... Treat younger men as brothers, older women as mothers, and younger women as sisters, <u>with absolute purity</u>."*
> ~ 1 Timothy 4:12, 5:1b-2 (NIV)

And yes, sometimes we defraud or flirt without even knowing it! That's why accountability is so important. It has always been my desire to be honest and open with the guys I know. I love having friendships with guys without having to deal with the romantic side of things! ☺ Sometimes it's hard, but it *can* be done.

I have many good friends of the opposite gender who I can honestly say I view as my brothers (and in Christ, they are)! We can enjoy spending time together as friends in a group setting. One should always be cautious of close friendships with someone of the opposite sex. We must constantly be evaluating our motives behind such relationships.

Modesty

This issue is especially important in light of flirting and defrauding, because dressing modestly is a *huge* part of our responsibility to the guys around us! So, what exactly *is* modesty?

- **Modesty:** *Propriety (standard of right) in dress and behavior.*

Basically, this is not wearing any item of clothing that draws attention to one or more parts of your body. Please, girls! This is so very important. I know many guys who have told me that they wish they could help girls understand what dressing inappropriately does to them. Listen to the perspective of Joshua Harris from his book, *I Kissed Dating Goodbye:*

> *"You may not realize this, but we guys most commonly struggle with our eyes. I think many girls are innocently unaware of the difficulty a guy has in remaining pure when looking at a girl who is dressed immodestly. Now I don't want to dictate your wardrobe, but honestly speaking, I would be blessed if girls considered more than fashion when shopping for clothes. Yes, guys are responsible for maintaining self-control, but you may help by refusing to wear clothing designed to attract attention to your body. I know the world tells you that if you have a nice body, you should show it off. And we men have only helped to feed this mentality. But I think you can play a part in reversing this trend. I know many girls who would look great in shorter skirts or tighter blouses, and they know it. But they choose to dress modestly. They take the responsibility of guarding their brother's eyes. To these women and others like them, I am grateful."*

Let's open the Scriptures and see what God has to say about modesty... ☺

"I also want women to dress modestly, with decency and propriety, not with braided hair or gold or pearls or expensive clothes, but with good deeds, appropriate for women who profess to worship God." ~ 1 Timothy 2:9-10 (NIV)

"The aged women likewise, that they be in behavior as becometh holiness, not false accusers, not given to much wine, teachers of good things; That they may teach the young women to be sober, to love their husbands, to love their children, to be discreet, chaste, keepers at home, good, obedient to their own husbands, that the Word of God be not blasphemed." ~ Titus 2:3-5 (KJV)

In the Greek, "discreet" means: *One who has a sound mind; a person who limits his own freedom and ability with proper thinking; demonstrating self-control with the proper restraints on all the passions and desires; to prudently restrict one's desires.* "Chaste" means: *Clean, innocent, modest, perfect, pure.*

"Therefore, as God's chosen people, holy and dearly loved, clothe yourselves with compassion, kindness, humility, gentleness and patience." ~ Colossian 3:12 (NIV)

These verses tell us that modesty on the *inside* is just as important as modesty on the *outside!* It is a standard of right that we demonstrate by refusing to defraud our brothers in Christ in any way. When a girl is modest inside, the outward appearance of modesty will be a natural byproduct of what is in her heart. Pastor C.J. Mahaney has this to say on the subject:

"Any discussion of biblical modesty begins with the heart, not the hemline... The humble Christian woman who understands this passage [1 Tim. 2:9-10] will have a wardrobe that expresses self-control, moderation, and restraint. What she wears will demonstrate that she lives with a settled resistance to the ceaseless pull of the world. She will dress to show the grace and beauty of womanhood and to reveal a humble heart — not to call attention to herself, flaunt her beauty, impress her peers, or allure men sexually."

Why not ask someone you trust, like your brothers, your dad, or your mother what they think you can do to help guard the eyes and hearts of the men around you? I have always been amazed and blessed by the advice of my family in regard to my wardrobe! My job here is not to tell you what specific articles of clothing you should or shouldn't wear. This is another area that must be between you, God, and your parents.

> **Take a moment to stop and search your own heart!**
>
> **Evaluate your wardrobe from the *Lord's* perspective.**
>
> **If you were to take Jesus Christ shopping with you,**
>
> **do you think He would be happy with your**
>
> **choices in clothing?**

And girls, I am not without my own failures in this area. ☹ We must pray for each other and for our brothers in Christ that we will follow God in this. Proverbs 5:3, 6:24-25 & 7:21 speak on the wayward woman and what the consequences of her actions are. These are examples of what we should stay as far away from as possible. Let's be Proverbs 31 women instead! ☺ Jesus set such a high standard of right in all He did. Shouldn't our motivation always be to live up to *His* standard? Don't let yourself get discouraged trying to live up to it!

*Realize that all you have to do is ask for **His** help and try your best.*
Let Jesus do the rest. ☺

> "How does a woman discern the sometimes fine line between
> proper dress and dressing to be the center of attention?
> The answer starts in the intent of the heart.
> A woman should examine her motives and goals for the way she dresses.
> Is her intent to show the grace and beauty of womanhood?
> Is it to reveal a humble heart devoted to worshipping God?
> Or is it to call attention to herself and flaunt her beauty?
> Or worse, to attempt to lure men sexually?
> A woman who focuses on worshipping God will consider carefully how
> she is dressed, because her heart will dictate her wardrobe and appearance."
>
> ~ *Pastor John MacArthur*

Should a girl date, court, or do something entirely different?

When I was younger, I heard a lot of discussion between Christians about whether or not we should be following dating or courtship rules in a relationship. It seemed to me there was a simple solution. Why not look it up in the Bible and see which way God likes best? So that's just what I did! And to my surprise, I discovered that the Bible doesn't mention either one! ☺ Instead, it talks about engagements and betrothals, like Mary and Joseph had in Matthew 1:18. But the question is, where does that leave us in this day and age? Well, I believe the answer to this question is found in one's *heart*.

> *"Search me, O God, and know my heart, try me, and know my thoughts:"*
> ~ *Psalm 139:23 (KJV)*
>
> *"Keep thy heart with all diligence: for out of it are the issues of life."*
> ~ *Proverbs 4:23 (KJV)*

I think it's not as important *what* you call the relationship, as it is the motive of your heart behind the relationship. If a girl's motive (be it through courtship or dating) is simply to achieve security, enjoyment, and fulfillment, then her heart is wrong! As Christians, our hearts belong to God. Our ultimate security, enjoyment, and fulfillment must come from *Him* and no one else. Nothing and no one should get in the way. ☺

So does that mean it's wrong to date or court? No, of course not. ☺ When the time comes to think about these issues, it really is a matter of much prayer, seeking wisdom from the Lord and others, as well as timing. For example, God has currently called me to a very full life of ministry and service to Him. For me, a relationship with a guy at this time would only serve as a distraction from what God has for me. Will it always be this way? Only God knows!! But, that is just where the Lord has me right now.

> *"Let every man [or woman] abide in the same calling wherein he was called."*
> ~*1 Corinthians 7:20 (KJV)*

Okay, girls, it's *your* turn now! Roll up those sleeves of yours, hold your head high and bring out the trusty ol' magnifying glass, because it's time for a Spiritual Evaluation!! ☺ 2 Corinthians 13:5 says, *"Examine <u>yourselves</u> to see whether you are in the faith..."* (NIV) So, please go right ahead and ask yourself the questions below:

> ➤ *What is truly in my heart?*
> ➤ *Do I want to have a relationship with this guy simply for the pleasure of it?*
> ➤ *Am I placing his needs ahead of my own? (Philippians 2:3-4)*
> ➤ *Is this young man someone I could see myself marrying?*
> ➤ *Is this young man a strong Christian? (2 Corinthians 6:14)*
> ➤ *What do my "wise counselors" think of this relationship? (i.e. God, Mom, Dad, Pastor - Proverbs 12:15)*
> ➤ *Am I content to walk away from this relationship if the Lord wants me to?*
> ➤ *Would this relationship hinder my walk with the Lord or strengthen it?*

We are to serve the Lord *without* distraction! After searching your heart, can you truthfully say that having this relationship would help you better serve God, or would this simply be a distraction? Let me encourage you to listen carefully to His call on your life and be honest with yourself. Each person is different. Remember, God has different callings for different people. What has He called *you* to do?

> **Distract:**
> *To stir up or confuse with conflicting emotions or motives.*

What's a girl to do during her single years?

1. Remain physically pure. (1 Corinthians 6:12-13, 18-20)

"Save yourself for the one God has saved for you." This phrase is on a poster that has hung on the door of my bedroom for years. Every day I look at it and am reminded to keep myself totally for the man my Savior is holding for me. God knows that is *not* an easy task! The temptations in this world are huge. But we have a verse of comfort in 1 Corinthians 10:13 that states: "There hath no temptation taken you but such as is common to man: but God is faithful, who will not suffer you to be tempted above that ye are able; but will with the temptation also make a way of escape, that ye may be able to bear it." (KJV)

2. Remain emotionally & mentally pure. (Philippians 4:8)

In Matthew 5:27-30 Jesus says that if we look at someone to lust after them, it is as if we have already committed sexual sin with them in our hearts. Wow. Let that one sink in! This is why we *must* feast our minds and hearts on the pure and wholesome things of the Lord. 2 Corinthians 10:5 says, "...bringing into captivity *every* thought to the obedience of Christ." (KJV) Ask the Lord to help you in this area! He's always willing and ready to help you. ☺

3. Remain focused on the Lord. (Psalm 73:25-26, 28)

God demonstrates time and time again that He wants to be our heart's only desire! Deuteronomy 6:5-6 says, "And thou shalt love the Lord thy God with *all* thine heart, and with *all* thy soul, and with *all* thy might. And these words, which I command thee this day, shall be in thine *heart*." (KJV) This principle of being focused on the Lord is becoming a daily discipline for me. How so? Well, let me share with you the journey that the Lord is bringing me through!

Several years ago I was shocked to discover that (once again ☺), my focus had been all-wrong. You see, getting married was just something I always assumed to be God's will for my life. I just knew how it would go! I would meet the perfect guy, fall in love, get married, have children, and spend the rest of my life growing old with him! Does this sound familiar to any of you? ☺

The Lord has begun to show me that being single is a completely and totally *awesome* thing! ☺ Of course, our culture doesn't necessarily agree! Even if you're single, it is expected that you get out there and date as many people as you can until you find the "one". But in reality, there is much to be said for staying single-minded! Single people can do so many different things for the Lord! Scripture speaks so plainly of the single person's freedom to serve the Lord in a completely different way than that of a married person. I have seen that while I am single, I should make the absolute most of it. Who knows what my future holds better than my Savior? And, who knows what's good for me better than my *Savior?* ☺

So I have committed myself to stay a single young woman striving to please the Lord wholeheartedly, without distraction, until Jesus shows me otherwise. And you know what? There is freedom!! I feel I don't have to play the dating game or be wondering constantly about a boyfriend, because I know in my heart that the timing isn't right. So I can get a relationship out of my head until the timing IS right! (<whispering> And by the way...in case you didn't know by now...God's timing in *always* perfect! ☺)

134

Now, it's not like I'm a recluse who hides under a rock avoiding all male contact! ☺ I still have friends that are guys, but I'm continually striving to keep my mind from checking out my "prospects." My goal concerning the guys in my life is to simply be their friend and sister in Christ. There is a freedom in being able to step back and say that I'm only looking for friendship and good fellowship among young people my own age. I am not ready to get married right now, so why should I go window-shopping?? ☺

I would encourage you to pray very hard about your future. Listen carefully to what Jesus has to say...and *obey.*

> "...*The unmarried woman careth for the things of the Lord, that she may be holy both in body and in spirit: but she that is married careth for the things of the world, how she may please her husband. And this I speak for your own profit; not that I may cast a snare upon you, but for that which is comely, and that ye may attend upon the Lord without* <u>distraction</u>." ~ *1 Corinthians 7:34b-35 (KJV)*

A Few Guy-Girl Suggestions:

Always treat a guy like you would treat your brother
*(Or the way you **should** treat your brother ☺).*

Be aware of the things you do that may lead a guy on.
(If you don't know, ask someone you trust!)

Be up front and honest with guys. (Prayerfully consider how honest you should
be with him. Now by all means don't lie, but sometimes it
*isn't necessary to tell **all** that you know!* ☺)

If a situation comes up that you are uncomfortable with,
or that you feel Jesus would be unhappy with,
do your best to get out of that situation as nicely as possible.

Remember, there is nothing wrong with being friends,
as long as that remains clear during the relationship! ☺

Consider what serving the Lord without distraction means to you.

We should remember that God gave us emotions and they are not bad things.
*It is what we choose to **DO** with those emotions that make them either right or wrong!* ☺

TIME TO THINK!

1. In your own words, what does it mean to "defraud"?

_____

_____

_____

_____

2. Does the way we dress affect the men around us? If yes, then how?

_____

_____

_____

_____

3. What is more important, inward modesty or outward modesty? Why?

_____

_____

_____

_____

4. Name a few of the things a girl should remember when having a guy as a friend:

_____

_____

_____

_____

What About Me?

1. Do I try to spur my brothers in Christ on to love and good deeds? Explain.

    _____

    _____

    _____

    _____

2. What are some practical ways that I can replace thoughts of guys?

    _____

    _____

    _____

3. Am I willing to live a single life if the Lord has asked me to? Why?

    _____

    _____

    _____

4. Do I think Jesus is happy with my choice in clothing? Why or why not?

    _____

    _____

    _____

5. Have I ever purposely done things to get the attention of the guys around me?

    _____

    _____

    _____

6. What are some distractions in my life that are keeping me from focusing on the Lord?

    _____

    _____

    _____

...𝓕𝒾𝓃𝒶𝓁 𝒬𝓊𝒾𝓏...

1. Name a few easy things a girl should do to remain healthy:

_____

_____

_____

2. How can bad posture reveal bad attitudes?

_____

_____

_____

_____

3. People with oily skin should use (circle all that apply):
    a. Extra moisturizing lotion
    b. Oil-free lotions
    c. Soap and water
    d. Alcohol on a cotton ball
    e. Facial powder

4. When you have a pimple, you should:
    a. Wash your face at least 5 times a day
    b. Wash your face once a week
    c. Wash your face at least 2 times a day
    d. Never wash your face...washing is for babies

5. Which is more important; inward beauty or outward beauty? Why?

_____

_____

6. What are the four different types of hair?
    1. _____
    2. _____
    3. _____
    4. _____

7. If you have frizzy hair, you should (circle all that apply):
    a. Always use a blow dryer on your hair
    b. Apply a small amount of lotion or smoothing gel to your hair
    c. Flip your head over and brush from underneath
    d. Backcomb, or tease your hair as often as possible
    e. Let your hair air dry occasionally

8. Simplicity is important when choosing a hairstyle.   True   False

9. A girl is never too young to start wearing makeup.   True   False

10. True beauty lies in the wearing of makeup.   True   False

11. When it comes to makeup, more is not necessarily better.   True   False

12. Name a few guidelines to follow when choosing clothing:

_____

_____

13. What makes someone a true friend?

_____

_____

_____

14. Young people are known for their respect and mannerly behavior when they're in public.
                                                                    True   False

15. Name 3 respectful things you can do while you're out in public:

_____

_____

_____

16. What are a few casual conversation topics?

_____

_____

_____

17. What is one principle from the Scriptures that is good to keep in mind when practicing good manners?

_____

18. God cares about how we act and the people we choose as friends.
                                                                    True   False

19. Name 3 of the character qualities Jesus Christ demonstrated:

    1._____

    2._____

    3._____

20. Circle 5 things about your life that cannot change:
    a. Clothing
    b. Nationality
    c. Gender
    d. Education level
    e. How much money you make
    f. Parents
    g. Siblings
    h. Where you live
    i. Time you die

21. Circle one the of the characteristics of a Prophet:
    a. Good with money
    b. Very decisive and firm
    c. Able to see the end result of a project

22. Exhorters are known for seeing and meeting people's needs.   True   False

23. Teachers are able to present truths systematically.   True   False

24. Describe the driving force behind the spiritual gift of Mercy:

_____

_____

_____

25. What are 3 ways you can become a blessing to those around you?

_____

_____

_____

26. What does "A stitch in time saves nine" mean?

_____

_____

27. Sorting clothes according to color before you wash them is unnecessary. True   False

28. One essential in the kitchen is a meat thermometer.   True   False

29. Match the definitions to the terms:

A. Scald
B. Glaze
C. Dice
D. Pare
E. Toss

a. To combine ingredients with a repeated lifting motion.
b. To heat liquid almost to a boil, until bubbles begin to form around the edges.
c. To gently remove the outermost skin of a fruit or vegetable.
d. To coat foods with glossy mixtures, such as jellies or sauces.
e. To cut into very small pieces, usually about 1/2 inch.

30. God gives us trials because He likes to watch us suffer.   True   False

31. God cares about the way we respond to every circumstance that comes into our lives.
                                                                            True   False

32. Name 2 things the Bible likens testing and trials to:

_____

_____

33. Name 2 reasons why God brings trials into our lives:

_____

_____

34. What does it mean to "flirt"?

_____

_____

_____

35. How can a girl demonstrate modesty on the inside & the outside?

_____

_____

_____

_____

36. What does serving the Lord without distraction mean to *you*?

_____

_____

_____

_____

Dear Friend,

WOW!! You made it all the way through this course. I'm impressed! ☺ I pray that this time has been meaningful and that you will be able to come away from this having learned something. Rest assured that my prayers are still with you as you tackle the road ahead!!

When all else fails, never forget that *God loves you and He has a wonderful plan for your life!* You need only to listen and be patient. He will tell you what to do. ☺

So, why not take some time to review what we've discussed in this course? There is room on the next two pages for you to do just that. The first page is between you and the Lord. Take a personal look into your heart, searching it thoroughly to see what is truly inside. The second page is a survey you can fill out. There is room here for you to write down some more general things that you have learned from taking this course. After you fill out this page, tear it out and send it to me! I would love to hear in your own words how the Lord is working in your life. ☺

If there is one thing you could take away from this course, I pray it would be that you would realize how *vital* a relationship with Jesus Christ truly is. May you find peace, love, joy, and fulfillment in Him! ☺

Take care and may GOD RICHLY BLESS YOU!

Myklin
2 Corinthians
12:9-10
♡

> *"Charm is deceptive, and beauty is fleeting; but a woman who fears the Lord is to be praised." ~ Proverbs 31:30 (NIV)*

143

As We Finish...

➤   Turn back to page 6 of this book and see what you wrote as you were beginning this journey through *What Every Girl Should Know.* Now that you've completed this entire study, take a few minutes to think about what we've discussed here.

➤   What have you learned? How near are you to the goals that you set for yourself in the beginning? What are some new goals you would like to strive for in the days ahead?

➤   Write your thoughts down about what you've learned from this course in the space below. Perhaps you need to ask the Lord to help you with some area of your life. Please just be still and hear what He may be saying to your ♥.

_____

_____

_____

_____

_____

_____

_____

_____

What Every Girl Should Know (WEGSK)
<u>Completion Survey</u>

- **I am a:** ☐ Student ☐ Mother ☐ Mentor ☐ Other:_____

- **I used WEGSK in:** ☐ Personal study ☐ One-on-one study ☐ Group ☐ Other:_____

- **Did you enjoy going through WEGSK? Why or why not?**

- **What was your favorite part?**

- **Are you going to make changes in your life because of something you learned? What kind of changes? (Example: I am asking God to help me read my Bible at least 5 minutes every day.)**

- **Would you recommend this to others? Why or why not?**

- **What would you say to someone who is considering going through WEGSK?**

- **Other comments:**

- **Do you mind if I use your testimony to encourage others?**   Yes   No

- **Would you like to remain anonymous?**   Yes   No

1. Name:_____   Age:_____

2. Address:_____

3. City/State/Zip:_____   E-mail:_____

P.S. Including your personal information on this survey is optional.
Rest assured that personal information submitted will be kept private! ☺

Send survey to: *What Every Girl Should Know*
PO Box 132
Maize, KS 67101-0312

For more information about Myklin's speaking ministry,
to purchase copies of her materials, or to share how the Lord has used this
resource in your life, feel free to write her at this address:

What Every Girl Should Know
PO Box 132
Maize, KS 67101-0132

Phone: (316) 729-1783
Fax: (253) 663-3720
whateverygirl@juno.com
http://www.whateverygirl.com